Don't Pee in the Wetsuit

Don't Pee in the Wetsuit

ക

A Worldwide Romp Through Grief, Laughter and Forgiveness

Michelle Elaine Kennedy

This book is based on true events. Some of the people in the book have been disguised and given different names, and I have changed a few facts to protect their identities. Other than that, everything in the book is true.

"The Journey Starts Here" translated in *The Forbidden Rumi* by Nevit O. Ergin and Will Johnson published by Inner Traditions International and Bear & Company, ©2006. All rights reserved. http://www.Innertraditions.com Reprinted with permission of publisher.

To my father,
for giving me strength, adventure and guts.

To my mother,
for teaching me how to love unconditionally.

To Shannon,
for sharing in "our" journey of a lifetime.

You shall stand by my side and look in the mirror with me.

~WALT WHITMAN

Cherri,
Thank you! I hope
for reading! you like it! ♡ Michelle

CHAPTER 1

❧

Run Away

I RIPPED MY clothes off and raced into the Pacific like someone lit my butt on fire. Sprinting neck and neck with Shannon, our feet pounded the wet sand until we dove in, splashed under the moon, and drifted out on our backs. The lukewarm waves vanished as gentle ripples cradled me. *Effortless*. The two of us absorbed the glory of that first night along the Western Coast of Costa Rica in silence: Shannon, the funniest person I knew, and me, the thirty-three-year-old who quit her career in broadcasting to travel the world.

Bobbing like a bottle in the sea, I shut my eyes and the front of his mangled truck appeared. Just like always, the hood curled up into broken metal fingers, clutching the windshield. A yellow tarp covered his body in the front seat. I longed to quit looking backward, but every time things got quiet, his beat-up Chevy showed up in my mind.

"Let's take our bras off!" Shannon yelled, snapping me back to the present.

I unhooked my bra and pulled it off. "Sweet!" I swung the bra around my finger. Apparently, I didn't mind the other travelers swimming nearby seeing my boobs up close. Tying the thing around my neck seemed like the smartest choice.

"You'll lose it that way, Dumb-Dumb. You'd better put that bra around your wrist."

"I got this!" I cinched the bra in a knot. "It's a bulbous bow tie!" I shook my jugs in the moonlight.

About thirty-seconds later, a wave crashed into my face. Nervous, I spit salt water and grabbed around my neck, only to find my bra had washed away. It was the only one I had since our luggage had been sent to Honduras by mistake. At that moment, I owned one pair of sweats that were surely being eaten by sand fleas on the beach, a dank tank top–thank God it was black–my underpants, and no bra. *Perfect. Just what I wanted, to not care and live in the moment. You got your wish, Michelle.*

Determined, I searched in the dark ocean for my slightly padded 36C. I figured I would definitely find it if I jerked my hands underwater fast enough. I heard buzzing around my head and noticed fireflies, dancing nearby. They reminded me to chill out and surrender. So, I counted my blessings, gave up, and plopped back down into floating-on-back-with-jugs-exposed-to-sky position, though I was mad I lost that bra. I bought it from Victoria's Secret and it cost me sixty bucks.

Lightning flickered next to a moon so full I wanted to reach up and wrap my arms around it. Thunder rolled and I felt grateful. We were celebrating a Wednesday night with no work to do and no responsibilities. I had only the ocean, my freedom, eleven countries, and 152 days of wandering to ponder. I wanted to scream for joy at the top of my lungs, but fear muted my lips.

Leaving my career as a television news reporter had been an out-of-body experience. The letting go, hurt. Even thousands of miles from home, I held on to things I could no longer smell or touch. Floating in the surf off Playa Grande Beach, I reminisced about the salty mist of the San Francisco Bay, wafting into my old apartment window. I held on to the way it had felt to lay in my bed and let the sun hit me like a cat curled up in a nap. I even heard the sound of my ex-boyfriend, Myles, and his footsteps approaching my door. I missed the constants, but acknowledged nothing was permanent.

Sunlight through my window was replaced with moonlight now, cascading across my braless body. No longer the cat curled up, waiting for something to happen, I'd finally escaped.

It was amazing we even made it to the West Coast of Costa Rica alive. After we landed at the San Jose Airport and got the smashing news that our luggage hadn't followed us, we paid our driver, Luis, to take us five hours north to our hotel. Looking at Luis, we never imagined he'd had aspirations to win the Indy 500. He hugged the winding roads with such ferocious tenacity that when the highway morphed from pavement to dirt, I thought we might just skid sideways right off a cliff.

Damp air blew through the open windows of the cab, sticking to my cheeks. Horses loped across rolling earth leading into rainforests packed with green and red quetzal birds. I wanted to take in every farm, every cow, and every smiling kid riding a bike home from school. I also wanted to eat exotic food and roll around with colorful men to my heart's content. For the first time in maybe forever, I wasn't in a hurry. I didn't have to be anywhere at any particular time, so I pushed my impatience out the window like an old list of things to do. Unfortunately, I had no idea how to sit comfortably with myself without doing something.

It took Luis the whole day to get us to Playa Grande. When we unstuck our sweaty legs from the white plastic seats, Shannon and I were greeted by growling howler monkeys lining the trees along the street. Our hotel property looked like a jungle with rooms interspersed inside of it. Hammocks swung from branches next to waves crashing in front of us. The humid air smelled like fermented mangos. The setting made me sleepy.

Our room reminded me of a college dorm with bunk beds stacked up. We walked in with miniature crabs following sideways behind us. It smelled moldy so we opened all the windows to air it out. We were also concerned with our own smell since we had very few toiletries in our possession.

"Do my armpits smell?" Shannon did the pit sniff.

"No, they don't."

(Four hours later.)

"Hey, do I stink? Like in the region of armpit?" I waved my shirt around my body as a test.

"No, you seriously don't."

"Unsavory?"

"No, seriously."

We also had repeated discussions about our lost luggage.

"This is real. What if our clothes never come?" Shannon looked down at her outfit for the fiftieth time.

"They have to come."

"Dude, I'm not sure I can wear these sweats for one more second."

"At least you have a bra."

On day two, Shannon and I spent three hours on the beach, taking pictures of a tiny Elvis Presley doll I brought from home. My oldest and best friend, Jessica, gave him to me when we were kids. I packed him because I read this travel book that said to bring something that reminded you of home. Tiny E was just one of my favorite silly possessions. He was the size of a Barbie doll and wore khakis, a bolo tie, and a pink and white checkered blazer. One of his saddle shoes had gone missing for about a decade, but miraculously, I found it in a drawer right before we left and put it back on Tiny E's foot.

"Now that foot is huuuge," I told him in my best Nicolas-Cage-impersonating-Elvis-Presley voice. Back in the early nineties, Cage used to do this skit on *Saturday Night Live* where he played Tiny Elvis Presley. The skits involved Tiny Elvis's friends driving him around town while Elvis commented on everything being "huuuge." In each scene, Cage, who was dressed as Elvis and had been shrunken down by the camera, would sit on dashboards and counter tops, saying things like, "Now look at that salt shaker. That is huuuge." I'm sure that's where my obsession with Tiny E began.

We wedged Tiny E's feet in the sand and captured Playa Grande Beach behind him. Then, we sat him on a log and watched tourists walk by, perplexed. Tiny E balanced on one foot and waved to people, or at least that's what it looked like when I put his hand in the sky.

"Jam him in the sand closer to the waves," Shannon suggested.

"What if I put him on my shoulder and gaze out all inquisitively?"
"Give me the camera."

Shannon was like that—full of ideas, light, and laughter. Her dirty-blond hair blew into the air as she positioned the King on my shoulder. Her eyes matched the color of the sky and she was the epitome of the girl next door. She was a spitfire—smart and beautiful, even without a stitch of makeup. I'd barely known my travel partner when we'd agreed to take the trip, but we believed we had enough in common to handle it and have a blast.

❦

Shannon and I climbed the career ladder for ten years before we met. She worked her way through law school and landed a job at a top firm in San Francisco, while I paid my dues at four different television stations to score a reporting and anchoring position, also in San Francisco. We'd never collected larger pay-checks, nor had we ever lived in a more unparalleled city. Around that same time, Shannon and I also realized we weren't entirely happy with our lives.

It was strange and sad to realize that my prestigious job didn't complete my life. People's faces used to light up when I'd tell them to watch me on television.

Viewers recognized me and guys thought my job was cool. A rush of pride consumed me when I visualized their reaction to seeing me holding the microphone. *Ego.* Television fed my self-esteem and it took a long time for me to release that attachment.

Shannon's legal career fed her self-esteem, too, but she decided she needed a change at the same time I did. We agreed over Gmail Chat that we should spend the next several months saving money and planning our six-month adventure. Actual Gchat excerpt below:

> **Michelle**: *I seriously just need to quit everything and go to the beach for like 6 months.*
> **Shannon**: *I am in Rutsville too. I want to take off too, just pack all my shit up, put it in storage and go.*

Ecstatic and terrified, Shannon and I often called each other in a panic before we left.

"I'm freaking out. What do we go back to? What if we run out of money?" she asked through tears one night.

These were the insecurities we discussed regularly. Our trepidation ran so deep, it often bled into other anxieties that had nothing to do with traveling. The whopper, of course, was the holy grail of thirty-something girl questions: "What if no one ever really loves me and wants to marry me?"

I calmed Shannon down when she got scared, just as she did for me. If we had one feeling in common, it was excitement wrapped around paralyzing fear.

The year was 2009 and our country had fallen deep into a recession. Most people thought we were nuts for dropping everything to travel.

"You will never find a job when you get back. You guys are crazy," our friends repeatedly told us.

We fully understood their concerns. The two of us just believed everything would work out. We'd put ourselves through graduate school and had worked our asses off in our respective careers. Shannon and I knew how to achieve goals and believed whole-heartedly we were capable of taking care of ourselves when we got back home, so we didn't listen to anyone and continued brainstorming our itinerary.

We lounged at the same café, night after night, on Chestnut Street, writing in notebooks stained with red wine glass circles. We planned to leave in July and travel through Christmas to Costa Rica, Ireland, Scotland, Portugal, Spain, Croatia, Italy, Australia, New Zealand, Indonesia, and Thailand.

The decision had come easily. For some reason, we wanted to explore the same places and there wasn't any debate about it. We figured arguments were bound to come on the trip—and they did—but there weren't any before that.

⚭

People, stepping over piles of seaweed along the shore, snapped their own pictures of Tiny Elvis. Some asked what we were doing and we lied and told them the pictures were for a book. Our sunlit beachside photo shoot was ridiculous and we loved it. The photographs turned out so cool, with Tiny Elvis sitting on a little stick in front of waves crashing behind him and Tiny Elvis on my shoulder with his hand in my blond locks. When we tired of taking pictures, Shannon performed Chris Farley impressions to make me laugh.

One of my favorite things she did was a Chris Farley bit where he'd play this commentator named Bennett Brauer. Also a *Saturday Night Live* character, Brauer would come on the news set during the show to do commentary about something, but never got to the point. Instead, he'd make these dramatic quotation-fingered statements, listing all of his shortcomings.

"I don't wear deodorant! I frighten small children! I don't pee in the potty! I don't smell good!" she yelled, impersonating him.

Shannon also did this thing where she'd stick her butt out the back of her pants and bend down in a ridiculous yoga position. It might have been appropriately called "awkward pose." She didn't even care that people were walking by as she stuck two inches of her butt cheeks right out of her two-day-old sweat pants. I laughed and tried to take a picture, but she covered up just in time.

That day with Tiny Elvis was so simple, packed with the mindless distractions that matter like Farley impressions and asses hanging out of sandy drawers. Sometimes, when life is happening, I think we forget how important those dumb, fun times are.

I put Tiny Elvis on the nightstand next to me and fell asleep that night feeling joyful. The heat of Costa Rica and the idea of not having to go home for six months made me smile. The sounds of waves, crickets, and rogue crabs scurrying about the floor put me to sleep.

⚬⃫

I am struggling to decipher the scene on the television screen. I can see the twisted dog carrier in the bed of the pickup, but I'm not sure it's the right truck. There are dead ducks on the ground beside the wheels. I squint and try to recognize the rest of the Chevy, but it's so smashed, I just don't know. A plastic license plate frame that reads, "California Waterfowl Association," dangles from the bumper. My face quivers. My heart pounds and I can't catch my breath.

⚬⃫

By day three in Costa Rica, I got exceptionally comfortable with dirty hair. After a couple of swims in the ocean, it curled into sticky ringlets. Eventually, you couldn't tell if it had been three or six days since my hair had tasted shampoo, so I stopped caring.

"Can you detect sand in my hair?" I asked Shannon.

"No. How long's it been?"

"I don't know. A few days (four)?" For the most part, I left it and scrubbed the sand out each time I went swimming. I came to the conclusion we don't need to wash our hair as much as we do.

Shannon and I ate rice and beans doused in this magical sauce called Salsa Lizano every night. Lizano is brown, full of sugar, and kind of vinegary. It's like Tapatio, but not as spicy and possibly as addictive as pizza. We got so obsessed with the stuff, we bought our own bottles and carried them around in our purses.

We drank copious amounts of Imperial beer with a caveman named Dan, who we met at the hotel bar, and his brute Marine friend, Peyton. Four years my junior, Peyton looked like a military man with tattoos, a buzzed haircut, and a square jaw. He told us he had come to Costa Rica from Iowa to relax before a deployment to Afghanistan.

"Aren't you scared?" I asked Peyton one night.

An iguana the size of a wiener dog shimmied past our table and mosquitoes attacked my ankles, despite the eight layers of Deet I'd smeared on my skin. A light breeze blew through the open-air bar out to endless ocean, caressing the shore below us. I tried to look sexy while scratching the welts on my shins.

"No. I'm excited to serve my country. I come from a military family. It's in our blood."

"Well, if I was your family, I'd miss you." Cut to sex scene… *Okay, not quite. Give me a second.*

"You know who you look like?" He was going to say Michelle Williams, LeAnn Rimes, or, "Renee Zellweger, but when she was in *Jerry Maguire*. You know, you've got the blond hair, the squinty eyes, and the big lips."

I got that, too.

"You know who you look like? That Swedish guy, Dolph Lundgren, from *Rocky IV*, but cuter and with his head shaved." *Sex scene within reach.*

Peyton and I debated politics, flirted, and drank beer for a couple hours. His blue eyes flickered in the moonlight. I coveted his muscular arms and massive shoulders. I wondered if he could pick me up with little effort. I also wondered if he could gently slam me against the wall whilst sucking my face off. His ivory teeth gleamed next to the lights of the candles lit along the bar.

When he finally asked if I wanted a tour of his room, I grabbed Peyton's hand and saluted him. "Yes, Sir!"

Peyton shook his head and laughed. A send-off seemed fitting; I did it for my country.

Before we got down to business, Peyton tackled a crab, frantically scuttling across the floor of his room. He tried to hit the crab with his flip-flop, but only hooked its arm in the rubber sole of his shoe. He held up the sandal to reveal only the crab's pincher sticking out.

"I got him! Sort of…" The rest of the crab tick, tick, ticked away. We laughed and sunk into Peyton's mattress.

Dolph and I rolled around on his tiny bed with sand stuck to the sheets. Mediocre at best, our sex did not rule. It felt like a Guinness Book of Records speed contest. As my bobble head whacked against the tiny headboard, I wondered if traffic school might be more fun.

I often regret the one-night stand because the same thing always happens: It gets all hot and heavy and then I remember A) I don't know this dude; B) It's so hard for me to truly enjoy this with a stranger; C) How can I escape so I can sleep in my own bed? and D) When am I going to fully accept that it's the connection I seek, not the act of sex? I do it because I'm using him to fill a gigantic void.

For a moment, while we tasted each other and melded our bodies into one, I almost believed I was connected and whole, but the second we merged, I felt small and like I was in the wrong place. He was literally inside of my body, and I wanted to climb out of my skin and run away.

When I'm with someone I care about, sex rules, but with a stranger, I can't get out of my head long enough to enjoy myself. I wish I could turn off my thoughts and really get into it, but I can't. Despite this, I go back and try again and again.

I reluctantly slept in Dolph's room. As he held onto me, snoring into my neck, I thought about that thing where you chew your arm off to escape. Mostly, I stared out the window at the moon and dozed off. When I woke, he tried to reinsert jackhammer and I made up some lame excuse to get out of there (had to wash my hair). I said goodbye, skipped to our room, and fell back to sleep below Shannon on the bottom bunk.

❧

Shannon, me, and our bare boobs floated for what seemed like an hour the night I lost my bra. We actually drifted about a quarter mile from our clothes, which made it extra awesome walking back down the beach–Shannon in her bra and underwear and me holding one boob in each hand–through groups of partygoers parked in the sand along the coastline.

"Hellooo. Hello everyone. How's it goin?" I would've waved, but my hands were occupied.

"Beautiful night. Beautiful night, yes?" Shannon twiddled her fingers at them.

The fireflies followed us with spirited flashes. I thought I saw my bra. It was seaweed.

Plopping down in the sand next to my sticky clothes, I lay on my back, listening to the tide smack into the shore. A light rain gently washed my face. Wind blew through my hair and I suddenly smelled the bourbon, seeping from his pores. A wave crashed and I heard his bellowing laughter. I closed my eyes and saw him kissing my forehead, then screaming in my face. I thought that if I left my life, I could avoid thinking about the thing that hurt the worst. *No such luck*. I needed to acknowledge the invisible travel partner I'd brought with me on that trip of a lifetime.

For years, I'd tried to forget the accident, our fights, and our highs and lows. I longed to escape and stop missing him, but now that I'd found my way to paradise, my father made his presence known in the sand beside me. He was there, forcing me to face him and the rollercoaster relationship we never got the chance to fix.

CHAPTER 2

∽

Ducks on the Freeway

RUNNING LATE AS usual, I couldn't find the blazer to match my blue pinstriped pants suit. Raindrops pounded the front window of the house as I darted around, searching through every closet. Each time I passed the television in the living room, I caught snippets of details on a multi-car accident on I-5 in Sacramento, California.

It was the morning of October 25, 2000. I was the new freelance night-side reporter at FOX40 TV and wondered if the road closures surrounding the crash would make me even later to work. Flustered, I stopped to watch a reporter announce that an entire section of the interstate had been shut down. Cars sat motionless in both directions because a semi-truck had hydroplaned at full speed across the median into another semi and several cars on the other side of the freeway. The reporter on the screen said someone's black dog had died in the crash after CHP officers tried to revive it.

"The backup is expected to continue through the night as highway patrol investigators comb through the scene in an effort to find out what happened. We do know at least two people have died in the accident and several more have been transported to the hospital."

One thing ran through my mind as I sifted through coat hangers—I would be sent out to do live shots on the crash for the next eight hours.

I'd been a reporter for about three years and car accidents were my nemesis. Those assignments were always so frightening—sometimes bodies would lie mere feet from me, beneath yellow death tarps. Sometimes, a family member would show up in a dramatic rush, only to hear the bad news and hit the ground, wailing. Accidents were the absolute worst. They were dark and depressing, but as the night-side reporter on duty, I didn't have much of a choice as to what story I'd cover. Sure of my fate, I finally found the blazer, put on my comfortable "car accident shoes," grabbed all the rest of my stuff, and flew out the door.

I knew the road closures would make everyone late that day; at least that was the excuse I'd planned to use for myself. With both sides of the freeway blocked, I opted to take the side streets, which helped a little. I couldn't drive fast, though, because sewers were flooded and many streets were submerged under several inches of rainwater.

When I finally arrived at the television station, thirty-minutes late, I jogged in to find several television sets in the newsroom, blaring updates on the accident. It's common for newsrooms to have multiple televisions going simultaneously so the competition, and what stories they're covering, are playing at all times. The room consisted of twenty square cubicles where reporters sat, vacillating between typing scripts and watching the accident coverage on the monitors above them.

Each screen showed different angles of trucks snarled together and a small red Volvo, teetering on its side. Rain drenched the pavement between investigators poking through the wreckage with flashlights. The scene hadn't changed much from earlier in the day; the accident still looked gnarly.

I turned away from the monitors and saw my news director stomp into the bullpen.

"You're late, Kennedy! Get ready because we're about to send you out there. Just need to see what the other reporter at the scene got first."

I sat down at the assignment desk where my friend, Jen, ate nachos with one hand and poked her computer keys with the other. She managed the desk and told reporters where to go and when. "Hey! Can I have some?"

"Sure. How are you? How is it living with Kasey?"

I stuck my fingers in, grabbed a chip full of cheese and beans, and caught Jen up on my life. She and I had worked together at another television station in Chico, California, and we had always gotten along well. She was my height—five feet, eight inches—with blond hair and big green eyes. Despite the chaos of television news, she always wore a smile and I adored her for that.

"It's nice. I mean, I'm not sure I should have moved in with him so fast, but he's good to me and his house is awesome." Truthfully, I was being lazy when I left Chico to move to Sacramento. Instead of doing the grownup thing, which would have involved finding a place of my own, I'd suggested moving in together and Kasey said yes. I'd sort of invited myself. We'd only been dating for six months, so I probably should have held off on taking such a big step so quickly.

"Well, he is super nice to you and you guys have a good time, so maybe it's a blessing and you just don't know it yet."

She was right. I grabbed another chip and shoved it in my mouth. "That accident blows. Am I covering it or are they gonna keep Victoria out there?" Victoria was the reporter who had been at the scene all day.

"It depends on if they open the freeway back up. If it opens soon, she could package it for the eleven o'clock show and we'll put you on something else. If you had been on time today, Missy, you would have been sent, but they kept Victoria out there because you weren't here yet. For now, hang out and file through the story log and the other stuff happening tonight to see if you like any of those stories better."

"I really am sorry for being late, but from what I'm hearing, you believe my punctuality problem might have actually helped me for once?" We giggled. I grabbed one last chip and headed back to my desk. Sitting down, I recognized my friend, Mike, doing a live shot for the competing NBC station on a monitor in front of me.

Fire truck lights flickered behind him as he spoke. "We do have some new details on the accident victims. According to the CHP, a fifty-year-old duck hunter from the small town of Lodi, died in the crash and there are ducks strewn all over the freeway. Until the next of kin has been notified, the CHP cannot release his name."

Trembling, I watched Mike toss back to the anchor who went on to another facet of the accident. My panicked reflection stared back at me in the monitor and life stopped. Paralyzing intuition punched holes in my heart. That was the moment when everything changed.

"Wait. Oh, my God..."

A Lodi native, my dad played hooky from work on Wednesdays to go duck hunting. It was Wednesday. *Could the ducks on the freeway be the ones he'd shot that day?* My heartbeat canceled out the room. *Was the dead dog they couldn't revive my dad's hunting dog, Boots?*

Without thinking, I picked up my desk phone and called my dad's car phone. Busy. Not good. I called again and got the same thing. Back then, none of us had cell phones; Dad's car phone was a novelty item.

Jen had walked away from the assignment desk, so I approached the evening executive producer, Kevin. My voice cracked. "Kevin?"

"What's up?" He didn't look up from his keyboard.

"I'm really... afraid that the guy who died in that accident is my father." The words felt like razors rolling off my tongue. Each one slid out more excruciating than the next. I stood there, waiting, shaking, and shrinking into myself.

"Wait. Why do you think it's your dad? They haven't released the names of the dead because they haven't notified the next of kin."

I could tell he didn't want me to be right; he practically argued with me. "I know. I'm telling you, I think I'm the next of kin. Can someone call the CHP?"

"They won't release the name before—"

"What's the number, Kevin?" As Kevin's fingers fumbled through his Rolodex, I looked up and saw Jen return to her post. She would help me faster. In tears, I ran to her. "Jen, you have to help me."

"What's going on?"

I told her what I told Kevin while he and the rest of the people in the news-room stared at me.

She picked up the phone to call the CHP number she knew by heart.

Disoriented, I slow-motioned it back to my desk and dialed my older broth-er Ryan's number.

"What up, beaaach?" His jovial manner burst through the phone.

"I think Dad might have died in that accident." I choked on the words. I didn't want to scare my brother. I also felt self-conscious because about fifteen people were staring at me.

"You mean the one on I-5 with the semi-trucks?" Ryan worked in sales and had just returned home after being stuck in the accident backup all day. He didn't want to believe me, either. *Who would?* I told him the whole story and he hung up the phone to call my dad and stepmother.

I got ahold of her at work. After I told her the details, she said it was prob-ably a misunderstanding and hung up to call the CHP.

At that point, the station general manager showed up to take me out of the newsroom. "We're going to figure this out, Michelle," she assured me while ushering me out of the room. "While we do, why don't we go upstairs (so you don't totally freak out when you find out your dad is for sure dead)?"

On our way out of the newsroom, Victoria, the reporter who had been covering the accident, rushed in, holding a videotape in the air.

"I have fresh video of the accident scene. Who's editing this?"

By that point, the entire newsroom knew what was going on. My face was red and I felt embarrassed, but didn't care. I walked toward her. "Victoria, you gotta give me that tape. I think my dad was in the accident and I need to see it. Now!" I grabbed the tape before she could answer.

"No. Only two people died. There's no way..." She watched me speed away.

I could tell she didn't want me to see the twisted scene that used to be sev-eral intact cars, two semi-trucks, and my living father. Gathering my courage, I popped the tape into a deck in an editing bay nearby and scrolled through the footage. Each frame revealed a different wrecked car, flashing lights, body bags, rain, and investigators standing around it all. As I scrolled, my co-workers stood shoulder-to-shoulder behind me, trying to decipher my reality. Those moments felt like someone had scooped my insides out with a shovel. I saw cops, helicopters, and more rain. That red Volvo, another semi, a roadblock, and… wait… a dog carrier strapped inside the bed of a mangled pickup.

There it was—my dad's Chevy, barely still attached to the plastic traveling doghouse.

That dog loved hanging out with my father. We had that in common. The dog carrier door dangled open, but Boots wasn't inside. The front of the truck arched up and back. Raindrops rolled like blood over shards of the front window, that was now a part of the front seat. My dad used to sit in that place. Sometimes I sat next to him. He also used to spin me around and kiss my forehead.

I could smell the inside of the truck as I stared at it in the monitor. I closed my eyes and heard Rush Limbaugh on the radio. *My dad laughs as he flicks his cigar out the driver's side window. He pats my head.* Life would be different now. I didn't know at that point how I would get through it. "That's it," I said to the air.

Everyone stared at me in silence. Nobody knew what to say.

From behind the crowd, Jen poked through with tears in her eyes. "I just got off the phone with the CHP. Is your dad's name Michael Kennedy?" Her eyes said she already knew the answer.

With that, I collapsed to my knees and screamed into them as people patted my back uncomfortably. My fists tensed and I wanted to run out of there, punching every person along the way. I wanted to jump off a cliff and fly as far away as I could. Thankfully, I got ahold of my boyfriend and he rushed over to take me to my Dad's house.

We arrived to find half the town already there. I couldn't understand how other people recognized the truck on the news and I never did until later. I guess I wasn't looking for it, at first. The CHP couldn't get ahold of any of us and neither could family friends, so they gathered at the house, not knowing what else to do. In such a small community, the door was always unlocked.

We drove up to find my ten-year-old half-brother, Dylan, standing at the end of our very long driveway. My father's twelve-acre property consisted of a gigantic two-story house, a barn, eleven acres of Cabernet grapes, a pasture full of sheep, a lake full of catfish in the back, and several fruit trees in the front.

Dylan was too big for it, but he ran and jumped into my arms when I got out of the car. My blond haired, hazel-eyed clone cried into my neck and told me he couldn't believe it.

For some reason, I said, "Don't worry. Nothing's going to change between us. We are always going to be together." Little did I know, that wasn't true. None of us kids knew that our worlds were about to change, even more drastically than they already had.

People hugged and drank inside the house. My little brother didn't let go of my hand. My dad's friends stared; they looked so sorry for us.

I wanted to run out the door and find my dad in the barn, plucking feathers off the ducks he'd shot. It would never again light up with his laughter and the sound of the football game playing on his dirty outside television set. He would never beam up at me, scruffy faced, and say, "Hi, honey! Get to work picking this mallard. I shot a limit today."

After everyone left, I sank into my dad's office chair and examined a canvas my friend's grandfather painted of my dad and all of his farmer buddies. My dad had appraised farmland for a living. In the picture, he was smiling ear to ear, with a full head of brown hair falling on to the corner of his thick glasses. They were square, like his jaw. He was wearing a gray flannel shirt with a duck embroidered above the left front pocket. A cigar peeked out the top of the other pocket.

The answering machine light blinked in front of me, so I pushed it.

"Mike, it's me. Jerry. Can you give me a call? I'm feeling scared about something and I want to hear from you. I'm watching the news... Just please, call me back."

"Mike, it's Bill. Call me back. I need to talk to you. Please, call me."

One by one, they all just wanted to ask, "Did you die today?"

According to witnesses, a semi-truck hydroplaned in the rain across the center divider and hit two cars on the other side. Another semi, coming in the opposite direction, then ran into them all. My father's truck got caught in the middle. His body was partially ejected.

My father's best friend and hunting partner told us he and my dad had taken different routes home from their hunting trip that day. His friend wanted to avoid the freeway, but my father, for some reason, chose to endure it. I'm sure that friend felt strange about the small decision that changed everything.

My older brother, Ryan, went to get some of my dad's belongings from the coroner, but all he came back with was my father's gold watch, which was now more like a third of a smashed-up watch. My dad's blood and arm hair was stuck in the grooves of the gold band. I guess the rest of the watch got cut off.

Every time I remember that watch, I want to scream. I want to hold my dad's hand and feel the whole watch around his wrist. I want to put my dad's hand on my face for one more second.

I want more time.

I wondered if it hurt and agonized over whether or not my father cried. They said he died instantly, but I don't know if that's true. I wanted to make him come back alive so I could take care of him and nurture him the way he had never known how to nurture me, which was strange and not strange at the same time. *Because I love you so much, you will eventually love me back the same way.* He was dead, and I still played that game.

Nights hurt the worst. The quiet suffocated me as despair pressed on my windpipe. Thankfully, I had my boyfriend and some longtime girlfriends there to support me. They'd play with my hair to make me go to sleep. Sometimes it worked and sometimes the tears fell like a leaky faucet no one knew how to fix. When I did fall asleep, I'd inevitably wake back up in a panic, hoping to God the accident wasn't real.

The truck flashed through my mind as I stared out of dark windows. I spent four nights at the house, wishing I could hear my dad's cowboy boots clip-clop though the garage door. Maybe if I prayed hard enough, I could make them come back.

I smelled his shirts and put one in a plastic bag. I'd bury my face in that bag until the shirt didn't smell like him anymore. I also took my dad's glasses. I put them on my face and tried to focus, but realized he hadn't been lying when he'd said he was legally blind. I sat in his chair in the barn, smelling the dirt and manure caked on the floor around his tractor. Looking out in the field, I wondered who would take care of the grapes I'd planted with him.

"These grapes are paying for your college education, sweetie."

I remembered squatting on my knees in the field to position milk cartons around the baby vines. The cartons would protect our plants from the Central Valley sun, rising in the east behind us. My dad showed me how to grow the grapes from planting to picking. I drove the tractor with him, pulled weeds, and almost cut my finger off pruning. Sometimes, I'd get so tired working in the vineyard, I'd lie on my back in the dirt to take a snooze.

It was easy to hide in eleven acres, but somehow, my dad always found me. "I see you! Now goddammit get up and move that rake. Those weeds aren't going to pick themselves, Michelle!"

I held the few pieces of jewelry my father gave me and read the only two cards he wrote to me. My dad was strong and not very sensitive, so those cards were like precious gold. I read them over and over:

I'm sorry if I am hard on you, but I only have you for one more year and I want to spend as much time with you as I can.

I had been seventeen then and he was talking about me going off to college. I wished I could go back and spend more time with him. I wanted one more hug and a chance to say things I never had the courage to express. Most of all, I wished I could go back to that morning and make him take the back roads.

CHAPTER 3

Make it Stop

OUR SUITCASES SHOWED up on day four. I put a bra on and we left to head south to Montezuma, Costa Rica. Another five-hour taxi ride later, we arrived to find the town as cute and quaint as other travelers had described. The downtown stretched for three blocks. Colorful storefronts—about seven in total—lined the street, reminding me of Italy, but quieter.

Shannon and I lounged like sloths every afternoon in that sweet little free-spirited village. Sweaty-faced, we sipped mango juice and watched hippies dance and sell homemade jewelry in the streets. In Montezuma, the clock arms didn't seem to move; the people there sauntered around in slow motion, us included.

We relaxed in hammocks, hanging in front of a café that made these fruit smoothies, possibly blessed by God himself, watching an earthy twenty-something swing long, white socks filled with sand in circles. Her friends strolled by and talked to her as she smiled and crisscrossed the socks in figure eights. Her blond hair was balled up in a dread-locked ponytail that looked like muddy ropes suffocating inside of a larger, even muddier rope. We made up dialogue we thought best matched the sock-swinging situation.

Person: "Heya, Judy. Whatcha dooooooin?"
Judy: "Oh, just swinging these socks around in circles."
Person: "What are you gonna do today, Judy?"
Judy: "Ohhh, I think I'll just swing these socks around in circles."

Shannon and I spent three solid afternoons reading and people-watching in our café hammocks. And man did we laugh. We laughed because we were happy and because there was nothing else we felt like doing. Sometimes, I'd get lost in Judy's sock show and daydream about our itinerary.

⚭

Even though Shannon and I agreed on our countries, we had specific reasons for picking each one. We'd chosen Costa Rica first because we wanted to lie on the beach for several weeks and release structure from our systems. We imagined swimming, eating, sleeping, and reading several books in between. So far, that plan was right on track.

Ireland would come second because our ancestors had come from there and I had always longed to see the stunning green hills of that country. Shannon had already traveled to Ireland, but she wanted to go back. Both of us knew it was some distance from Central America, but we needed to get up to Europe, anyway, and didn't mind the long flight.

We researched the concert schedules of our favorite bands in the hopes of connecting with one of them on our trip. By some miracle, U2 scheduled one of the first concerts of their 360° Tour in Scotland, so we planned to head there after Ireland to watch the show.

We also wanted to embrace the beaches and make friends with the food in Portugal and Spain, so we decided to travel from Portugal to the northern tip of San Sebastian, Spain next. The popular town looked magnificent in pictures and the food there was supposed to be delectable so, of course, I wanted to eat my way through.

Shannon's best friend, Brett, planned to meet us in Croatia; we'd also heard incredible things about the coastal towns there, so we put that next on our list. Both of us had already visited Italy, but Shannon's co-worker had raved to her about a dreamy villa situated in the middle of the glowing orange and green hills of Tuscany. The co-worker told her that old Italian women cook all day in the kitchen and before they feed you, you drink homemade wine and eat fresh olives from their trees. It sounded too good to be true, so we decided to go there after Croatia.

Next, we planned to travel to Australia to dive in the Great Barrier Reef and to see live kangaroos. My grandma told me New Zealand was her favorite country, and since she'd traveled to forty countries, I insisted we take her word for it and go there, too.

We decided to end the trip in Indonesia and Thailand. Shannon and I envisioned lying around in more hammocks and swimming in translucent waters. We also wanted to eat authentic Thai green curry for as many days as possible before we'd travel back home, so Thailand seemed like a perfect ending.

The two of us mapped out an idea of how long we wanted to stay in each country—about two to three weeks—and wondered if we'd stick to the plan. We wanted to keep things open in case we didn't like a country or wanted to stay longer in another. We would get on cheap hotel or hostel websites and book rooms for the new place right before we left the old one. We did buy the first two plane tickets ahead of time—one to Costa Rica and one to Ireland. Other than that, we agreed to book the rest of our flights and hotels as we went. At the time, plane tickets were pretty cheap and they didn't fluctuate much whether you booked them in advance or last-minute.

We got all the shots recommended for our desired destinations at the local immunization clinic, including hepatitis, typhoid, and polio. I also bought health insurance that would fly me home in the event I fell off a cliff or got bit by a rabid monkey.

❧

Our last night in Montezuma, we experienced an incident that both terrified and amused us. The evening kicked off with a ferocious thunderstorm that woke us up when it pummeled the roof of our hotel room. Crashing thunder sounded like colliding garbage trucks. Rain pounded and lightning flashed so brightly, it lit the room.

"Do you think it could catch this place on fire?" I asked Shannon.

"I don't know. What if there's a flood?"

"Can we get electrocuted?"

"Wait. Does that actually happen through a building?"

We white-knuckled our sheets above our chins and prayed the storm would pass; it finally did. About an hour later, our anxiety returned with a raucous thud. Two firm knocks on the wooden frame of my bed woke us again. We bolted up in the dark, half asleep and confused. In my stupor, I thought either someone was under the bed or a bat had gotten in the room.

"Seriously. What was that, Michelle?"

"I don't know. I'm freaking out."

"Well, look!"

"Okay. God!" I crept up and gingerly lifted my head around to the foot of the bed to make out a little checkered jacket and two tiny black shoes in the dark. How could the King have made it onto the floor all by himself?

"It's Tiny Elvis."

"What?"

It turned out Tiny Elvis had taken a tumble in the night. I'd set him up on a rumbling mini-fridge that sat on a table in front of my bed. He had fallen off the fridge and whacked my bed frame on the way down. When we realized what had happened, we laughed harder than the thunder roared.

We left Montezuma after four days, content that we hadn't slipped too far into non-responsibility land. Visiting Montezuma was like sliding down a pleasant wormhole; I'm sure Judy is still swinging those socks and the smoothies continue to flow there like the rain that comes every night.

The next day, we headed north to the mountain town of Arenal, situated in the northern/central part of Costa Rica. We had been told to hike around the Arenal volcano, where ants carry gigantic leaves on their backs and various monkey species swing from trees that tower above skinny dirt trails.

Another ferocious rainstorm met us at our hotel with "volcano view." Walking to the front office, an adorable black and brown puppy—who had come out of nowhere—chased after me. He tried to bite my shoe, so I ran away and slipped on the wet pavement. My butt hit the ground, and the puppy leapt into my lap. Shannon laughed so hard I thought she might pee. Maybe she did. I played with that dog for days.

The two of us got caught in several torrential rainstorms and trekked across bridges that swung over endless valleys. We took photos of leaves the size of bed sheets, hog-nosed pit vipers, and red and blue poisonous dart frogs. We climbed up to the volcano with a tour group and waited with nearly 200 people for something to happen. Sitting on a wet mountainside, we squinted, but all we could distinguish were some underwhelming plumes of smoke spiraling out of the mountain.

"Can you see lava?" we asked each other over and over again.

The answer continued to be, "No," until the sun went down enough for us to spot minute clumps of lava, bubbling around the sides of the volcano. The wimpy show lasted for a few minutes until it got too dark and the mosquitoes showed up. Exhausted, we loaded into the tour van for the hour-long journey home.

"Costa Rican massage!" our driver shouted through laughter as we bounced along the uneven road.

We finished our tour of Costa Rica with three days in a town on the country's southern tip called Mal Pais. Coconut trees lined the long dirt road to our hotel. The path unveiled yellow and black toucans, purple orchids, sugarcane, and bright green grass. Our wooden hut was tucked away by itself inside a circle of trees. Declaring it our plantation, we pretended the house was ours. I loved the crystal clear pool and our very own clothesline. The monkeys in the trees and the buzzing cicadas eased my mind.

Sipping beer by the pool, I thought about my friends back home. Four o'clock in Costa Rica means Happy Hour. At my old job, it represented panic hour. Our video news packages for the first evening newscast were due by five, and I felt my shoulders tense just thinking about it. Every day was the same. Would I get my story in on time? Would I nail my live shot? Would Myles call and tell me he missed me? I hated all of the stupid questions that didn't matter anymore. I felt guilty for thinking about the bad stuff and ashamed for not doing cartwheels over my luck.

❦

The last television station I worked at in San Francisco laid off dozens of people over my three years there. To save money, management decided that reporter/photographer teams weren't a necessity anymore and that one person should go out and do it all—shoot, interview, write, edit, and set up live shots.

For anyone who has never done this, the one-man-band operation blows. It isn't impossible to shoot and edit a story alone in one day, but there is a big difference between one person covering a story over the course of eight hours and one person covering several stories, teases, and story-versions for multiple shows in eight hours. My colleagues and I struggled with the latter and the results weren't spectacular.

Throughout my eleven-year career, I put together touching and artful pieces. I thoughtfully told stories about people overcoming obstacles, returning from war, and saving lives. I covered murder trials, hostage standoffs, and high-speed chases, as well as the President Obama and Governor Schwarzenegger elections. I even interviewed Vanilla Ice in his tour bus. I mean, how do you top that? Bottom line: The reality of the situation made me sad because I'd transitioned from caring about my work, to slapping pieces together as fast as I could, to survive.

Meanwhile, the station managers created more work and expected my co-workers and me to continue to fill the time slots. We all joked about being part of an experiment. Each time we all managed to meet our deadlines, we imagined the managers saying, "Let's see if they can handle even more." I entered the building every morning, eight-gallon cup of coffee in hand, saying to myself, "This is like walking into cancer. This place just IS cancer."

After a few years, I detached and lost much of my passion for television news. The business was evolving at a rapid and cheaper pace and I either needed to adapt or run. I'm not the type of person who sits around bitching about my situation for long, so I chose to escape.

A year before the trip, I convinced the station managers to switch my days off to Tuesdays and Thursdays. I then applied to San Francisco State University to earn a Master's degree in radio and television on my days off. My goal was to teach college students how to function as one-man-band reporters. I would have to find a balance between telling students about the positive points of the business—and yes, there are many—and the negative ones. If I came in hating on news, I would never get a teaching job.

Over the next year, I made my plan a reality. Just as soon as I got accepted and enrolled in classes, a part-time teaching position opened up in my department at SFSU. I applied, got in and felt so blessed that I did. The class was popular for undergrads in the broadcasting department and was precisely the type of course I wanted to teach.

BECA 660 is an advanced reporting course where students produce content for a thirty-minute newscast that airs on public access every week. Luckily, the class ran on my school days. At that time, I didn't have any days off; I was either at school or reporting for the station seven days a week.

Despite the crazy schedule, I instantly experienced more joy in teaching than I had for years working in news. The students' energy inspired me. I acted as news director, while each student played a role in the production process. Each week, one student produced, another did sports, someone did weather, and the rest either wrote or shot and edited pieces for the newscast.

I showed them how to stand up straight and get through their live shots with presence and pizazz. I fixed their hair and straightened their ties so they'd shine on camera. I taught them how to write in active voice and hook the viewer up front. Most importantly, I begged my students to really listen to interviewees so they wouldn't turn into robot reporters, only concerned with being on television.

Nervous as ever, my students ran around like mice those first weeks, trying to get it all done. They were so excited to create stories with solid writing and editing. I felt so proud, overseeing their first newscast, I almost cried watching it. I even bought them two extra-large pizzas for their last show. I fell in love with those kids, just as I did with the students I taught the next semester... and the next. I've stayed in touch with many, writing them letters of recommendation and reviewing their cover letters and resume reels. Segueing into teaching proved I could be happy doing something other than reporting. It changed my life and my perspective.

Determined to take a break before getting out of news and going into teaching full-time, I devised a plan to travel. At thirty-two, I had always wanted to venture away, but I'd spent so much time moving up in the news business, I'd never given myself the chance. In the midst of trying to figure out my exit strategy, the television station laid off another round of people and I got the ax. It made sense. My attitude toward the station, at that point, was terrible and I'm not surprised they wanted to get rid of me. I beamed as the company's accounting director wrote my severance check. It went right into the trip fund, so financially, it worked out perfectly. Shannon and I left a few months later.

Our second-to-last night in Costa Rica landed on a Sunday. The blues washed over me because I had to say goodbye to a place I really loved. At the same time, I felt embarrassed for already missing Costa Rica when we were headed straight for Ireland.

Shannon and I wandered in the gummy heat to the only open tavern in town. Our sundresses stuck to our bodies like cellophane.

A sign on the wall said Sunday was movie night. *True Romance,* a film about two people willing to do anything for love, played on a television nailed to the wall of the outside bar. Dozens of people lounged on stools around a square counter and several couches. Despite three ceiling fans spinning at full bore, everyone appeared to be on the verge of melting.

I'm not sure if it was the booze, the sultry air, or the onscreen chemistry between Patricia Arquette and Christian Slater, but something happened when I started conversing with the towheaded bartender, washing glasses behind the counter. His blue eyes leveled me as he pushed sun-bleached curls behind his ears and told me about his move to Costa Rica from North Dakota.

Charlie said he had gotten sick of everything. "I had to get out. I got tired of going to work every day and doing the same thing. I wanted to bartend and just do me, so here I am."

"What about your people? Do you miss them?" I asked.

"No. They aren't going anywhere." He tilted his head and leaned in, smirking. "Let's talk about the good stuff. What do you love? Who do you love? What are you reading? Do you write?"

How did he know?

"I am writing. It's heavy right now. I'll tell you later."

"I hope you do cuz I kind of want to hear everything."

Charlie told me about daily surfing trips that made him feel closer to nature and God. We talked about Radiohead and Jack Kerouac's writing. When I ordered another Sierra Nevada, Charlie pushed the beer out an inch, looked at it, and then hid it behind his back. He leaned in again. "You can't have this unless you kiss me."

I held his face in my hands. "I would have kissed you anyway."

With our lips softly resting against each other, we didn't move. Instead, Charlie and I hovered in that space, breathing each other in like nothing else existed. That quiet place—where everything stops—is my favorite. When we pulled back to take each other in, I rested my forehead against his. The question on my mind fell out of my mouth. "Were you running away from stuff when you came here?"

Am I talking to him or myself?

"I don't think so. Maybe. I don't know." He giggled. "Why is it wrong to want to spend all my time surfing and serving drinks? What are you running from, darlin'?"

Touché.

I suspected Charlie, who was thirty-eight, was escaping something in Costa Rica and that unavailable mysteriousness intrigued me. If I'm honest about anything, it's that I like to try to figure out the "un-figure-out-able." Unfortunately, that quest always leads to heartbreak and a "Dead End" sign.

I squelched my doubts and questions and continued kissing my new friend for the rest of the evening. He kept the bar open longer than usual so we could hang out. After Charlie closed up and locked the doors, we lay down on a couch against one of the sidewalls.

Charlie and I talked about big things, little things, favorite colors, and favorite people. Mostly, we just made out.

"It's impossible you kiss this good." Charlie said.

His grin lit the dark room. "I've been practicing for you on my hand."

We laughed. We were comfortable. We connected with an ease I rarely experienced. Chemistry permeated the air between us, sticking to sweaty shoulders and chests. In between kisses, I wished the clock would stop so I could spend more time with Charlie. He touched my face and held my hand. We snuggled and kissed some more until the sun rose like a bomb, forcing us off the couch. I didn't want to leave, but Shannon and I were headed to Dublin that morning, so Charlie escorted us back to the jungle hotel.

When we arrived at the plantation, Charlie and I settled on a lounge chair by the pool. The minutes passed like grains of sand slipping through my fingers. I tried to hold on to them, but couldn't. In our last hour, we dug deeper into our experiences with love and its companion, pain.

"What about your mom and dad?" I asked.

"My mom and I haven't spoken in three years. She is totally preoccupied with her life and doesn't involve herself much in mine." He pushed his hair back and paused. Charlie's square jaw outlined his chiseled face. "My father was executed for killing two people."

I stared at him, stunned into silence. I had never heard anything like that before and I didn't know what to say.

Did he really just say that?

Charlie looked out across the pool. Blank.

"I'm so sorry. Are you all right with it now?" I kissed his hand.

"I'm okay. He wasn't in my life then and he isn't now. He wasn't ever there."

I didn't know what else to do for Charlie except put my arms around him and share my own story. I told him about my dad and the circumstances surrounding his death. I told him about the watch and how terrified I had been. As the words came out of my mouth, tears streamed down Charlie's face. How could he weep for me? His story seemed so much worse, but then again, whose story is worse or better than someone else's? We all hurt. In those moments, his sorrow dissolved into mine.

"I want it to go away. I thought I was over it, but now I'm here on the coolest trip ever, and it throbs like it happened yesterday. I don't know how to make it go away. How do you make it stop?"

Charlie kissed my forehead and face and held me tight to his chest. "You can't make it stop until it's ready to be stopped, Michelle. You have to grieve and feel it. Be mad at him for leaving, love him, accept him, breathe in the excruciating details, and then let it all go. All you can do is keep trying, but if you don't try, it isn't going to get any better. You can't run anymore."

I took a deep breath and twisted one of Charlie's curls in my fingers, wishing I could hold on longer. I marveled over the attachment that formed in a matter of hours. I cried because I missed him already. I wished we could snuggle up in his bed for at least a week... or month...year.

Rubbing my nose over his neck, I recognized the infatuation, swirling inside me like fog about to be burnt by the sun. I wished so hard for more time, but our shuttle would arrive in an hour and Shannon and I weren't even packed. I wanted to hold on, but needed to let go, just like he said.

"I've never experienced a night like this before," I said.

"Me neither. These might be some of the sweetest moments I've ever spent with someone."

They were the moments I longed for—connected ones where two people smooth out each other's deepest scars... moments when I relate to another human being who actually sees me and relates back with common experiences and kisses on my cheeks. In this place, I am not damaged, complicated, or unlovable; I am appreciated for all I am.

Charlie pulled me close again, kissed me, and took my breath away. Then, he straightened up, grabbed my shoulders, and stared into my eyes. "Everything will be all right. You will get through this. Just don't quit." He embraced me one last time then stood and left my world. I watched him go and wondered what made me more depressed: death, loss, longing, or all of it smashed together.

After he vanished, I leapt up to chase him. In my bare feet, I ran as fast as I could down the dirt road. When I got to the end of the driveway, a mini dirt storm following behind me, I watched him walk away with his head down. Charlie wiped tears off his face and I couldn't breathe.

Nothing stays. I wanted to make him come back, but knew I couldn't.

You can't fix this one, Michelle. Fix yourself.

CHAPTER 4

❦

Where is He?

DUBLIN IS A colossal city full of rocky buildings and all the friendly people you could ever want to meet. The beer flows there like a raging river and pubs line the streets. We arrived in August, ready to do a keg stand on the city.

Shannon and I touched down in Ireland after three devilish flights. We found our tiny budget hotel after about thirty minutes of wrong-turn frustration and fell face first onto our bed with clothes and shoes still intact.

Our room didn't smell savory. A fluorescent overhead light flickered on and off above our heads, reminding me of Chief Bromden and his broom. The windows didn't have screens and with no air-conditioning, we were forced to keep them open, inviting mosquitoes to float in like wavy smoke monsters. A mysterious opening peeked through the bathroom ceiling and two little black sticks stuck out of it. Maybe a bat got wedged in there and died.

A stained white carpet obscured the floor around a mattress with springs protruding through the top like baby fingers. Finding *Oprah* on the television set things right again, at least for the next hour or so; Dane Cook was the guest.

Thankfully, we were able to nod off in the bed that barely fit us. Drifting off, I heard Dane doing an impression of Oprah and all the extravagant gifts she gives to her audience members.

"Everybody gets humpback whales!" Dane Cook screamed. "You get a humpback whale! You get a humpback whale!" The audience jumped out of their seats, laughing. Maybe some people fainted.

We laughed, rolled over, and fell asleep.

After we woke up that first night, we headed out to meet Shannon's friend, Aiden. The weather and layout of Dublin reminded me so much of San Francisco. Cars sped by the hordes of people, rushing like they were late for something. There were huge churches, universities, art, and statues everywhere.

We met Aiden in a pub called Quays Bar in the Temple Bar District. Although touristy, the place was quaint and easy to find. Shannon knew Aiden through friends in San Francisco. Originally from Dublin, the redheaded, blue-eyed Irishman had worked in San Francisco for a year until his visa ran out. It just so happened that the day before we got in, he was forced to come home to Dublin.

"I can't believe you guys did it," he kept telling us. "I can't believe you're here."

"You are our tour guide! Show us everything!" I grinned at him.

Aiden took us to Christ Church, a gorgeous cathedral in the heart of the city, the next day. The architecture there is rich and statues adorn the corners of the building. Aiden and Shannon opted not to go in, so I took some time alone inside. I sat by myself and smelled the incense, then prayed and thanked God for all my blessings and for getting me there safely. Still exhausted from jetlag, I dozed off in the second pew.

↫

I am sitting in my father's office chair the day he died, staring at his desk calendar. He has "duck hunting" written on Wednesday and a farmer's luncheon written on the following Friday. I pick up the phone to call Father Mike who'd baptized and confirmed me. I need him to make sense of my father's death and afterlife.

"Father Mike, what am I supposed to think? Dad said he didn't believe in anything. How should I visualize him now? He always said that when he died, he thought it was like falling asleep. He thought everything would just go dark. How can I imagine him being happy and at peace if he didn't even believe it was possible? Where is he?" Tears pour down my face.

"God will take care of him now, Michelle. Imagine God putting his arms around your dad the second your father gets there. He will show your dad the way and make him understand he wasn't right about death. It's a beautiful thing. God will take care of everything. Your dad is happy. He is at peace. You have to believe me."

⤸

I woke up, wondering if Father Mike was right. I don't think we can ever know for sure until we die ourselves.

That night, Aiden took us to one of his favorite pubs, the Brazen Head. We filed in and saw a long wooden bar full of mostly men, telling stories and carrying on. It smelled like stale beer inside and the men seemed tall and louder, compared to the guys back home. They were also friendlier than San Francisco lads. In Ireland, I truly believed I could be wearing pajamas with my retainer in, and if an Irish dude decided he wanted to talk to me, he'd chase me down the street. Men flirt everywhere, but in Ireland, they lay it on thick.

A boisterous crowd of burly guys, toasting, roasting, and cheering in the back corner, captured my attention. They must have caught me staring because one of them asked me to take a portrait of the group.

"What's this for?" I asked.

"We's having a stag pawty for me mate over der. I'm Duncan."

"Hi. I'm Michelle."

"Where's ya from?" His eyes lit up when I told him. Duncan said he liked Californians. He also told me he loved my dents (teeth).

The wolf pack consisted of eighteen firefighters. *I know, right?* All easy on the eyes, they were full of questions about our trip and America. My favorite guy ended up being giant Duncan. I liked his muscular arms, big teeth, warm smile, and energy, in that order.

"Yer boobs fake, are they?" Duncan asked about two minutes into our conversation.

I tried not to laugh. "No, they are very real."

"Ah, come on. Doesn't everybody in California have fake boobies?"

I probably should have reacted, but this guy was hot and smelled like Irish Spring. I do always pick the obnoxious, soapy-smelling ones.

Duncan might have been out there, but he wasn't stupid. I quickly found out he had a lot to say about the violent history surrounding his country. Between sips of beer, he told me about Ireland and Northern Ireland and explained the struggles his people had endured.

"Ya just don't know. It's still hard today. The Unionists just took North Ireland. Everybody knows all the best counties are up there and they took 'em."

It was fascinating to hear what I had read about and seen in movies from someone who actually lived there. I thought about my family who had migrated from Northern Ireland, the very place Duncan despised. I kept those details to myself.

At one point, Duncan took me down the street to show me the firehouse. I think he was just trying to show off the American girl to his co-workers and that was fine with me. The firehouse reminded me of the ones back home. So did the firefighters.

I wanted Duncan to grab my face and kiss me. I wished he would pounce.

Kiss me, Irish Spring. Distract me. Take me out of my thoughts. Nope.

"Now, when the alarm goes off, that is when we go right into action," Duncan said, jerking me out of my trance.

He showed me the trucks and fire pole, as if I was an ignoramus who knew nothing about fire stations, and I thought about Charlie. I wanted to be back in the heat with him lying next to me. I wanted to feel that rush again. I knew it was infatuation—something that always burned me in the end—but I still grabbed on for the thrill it provided. Truthfully, I wanted someone to be my equal partner, for once. Standing there, observing Duncan demonstrate how he puts his fire gear pants over his other pants, I wondered if I'd ever experienced full, reciprocal love with a boyfriend.

Duncan finished his presentation and stared at my chest. "Are ya sure they's real?" he asked again.

"Oh, for Christ's sake. Just feel." With that, I leaned forward, he pinched my boob, and we headed back to the bar.

"Yer right! They's real. Brilliant!"

I laughed and shook my head. "I'm happy for you, Duncan."

After Duncan got to second base–minus the kissing–I moved on to talking to the joker of the group. Blond Jack bounced around, telling jokes that only he laughed at, all the while punching his friends in the arm whenever he made a point about something. Jack worked feverishly to teach me the vilest of Irish slang.

"Did ya get your hole?" he asked.

"What does that mean? Like golfing?"

"No, sex! Like did you get the sex with da girl? That's what it means."

"Oh, okay. What else?"

"Langer up the gicker."

"Oh, sex again?"

"Nah. Up thee ass!" Serving as a roadblock, one of Jack's friends nudged in and introduced himself.

"That's a bad example of Irish men. He's ridiculous. Don't listen to him. I'm Colm."

I could tell Colm was the oldest of the bunch. Streaks of gray peeked through his brown hair and his belly stuck out as a symbol of the many beers I'm sure he'd consumed over the years. I thought Colm to be the most put together of the group; I would soon find out my impression of him missed the mark.

Colm and I chatted for about an hour. He told me about his marriage and how he didn't like his wife anymore. "Put it this way, we both see udder people, if ya know what I mean."

"What?"

"That's just the way it goes for us."

Colm told me he didn't fancy getting divorced because he and his wife owned property together. I felt sorry for him because of how miserable that sounded. The vibe changed a bit when I told Colm what I thought of the situation.

"Why be unhappy when you could be happy? Why make vows and cheat?"

"Because it's something we agree on. It's too hard to split it all up."

"But then there's no point in making a commitment. Don't you believe you can be happy with someone else or have you given up?"

"You just don't understand. You haven't been married."

I felt depressed, listening to him. Did I not understand? Is that what I had to look forward to? No way. "I don't believe this is the norm and I don't believe this is what you have to accept for your life. I just don't."

Colm shook his head, indicating his acceptance of the status quo. I took it as another reminder of what not to do in my life. I tried not to judge, but I did. I would never accept a situation like that; I'd rather be alone.

I left Colm and found Duncan again, but he was so drunk, he could barely stand up. We all agreed to meet at another bar, but by the time we got there, Duncan had headed home. I wasn't too upset about not kissing him. I'd rather kiss someone who could still see straight. Colm wasn't far behind him. He bobbed and weaved, his speech slurred.

"I'd like to fuck ya, though."

Of course, he would. I wasn't his wife. "No, thank you, Colm."

I joined Shannon and Aiden for a few more drinks before we found a Lebanese restaurant that served up the most delicious late-night chicken pancake pita things I'd ever tasted. Well, to be honest, I'd never tasted a Lebanese pancake before, so maybe that's why they were so exceptional. Vegetables and some mysterious sour cream sauce filled the cake. The flavors hypnotized me into obsessive thinking. "Do you think I could marry this pancake?" I asked Shannon and Aiden. "I don't think this pancake would cheat. I love this pancake. You's my pretty pancake," I told it.

"You crazy," Shannon said.

I left with a sour cream mustache on my face, wishing I had ordered a pancake to go. I'd like to go back to that restaurant. I should have written down the name.

We said goodbye to Aiden and slept like coma patients that night. I laughed when I thought about the firefighters. Those guys certainly entertained me with their antics and broad shoulders. I wondered if I would meet my husband in Ireland. Maybe I would, just not that night. I wondered what I wanted my husband to be like. The time had come to get a little more specific about that.

The next day, we headed to Galway, on a five-hour bus ride through the romantic, green hills you see in travel magazines. One of Ireland's most popular towns, Galway, sits along the western coast of the country and backs up to the River Corrib. Cows, sheep, and old men on tractors canvassed the landscape around us. Rain glistened on stacked hay bales and little streams, following us on the side of the road. I fell asleep on the bus and woke up thinking I was back in my hometown, Lodi, California. I had to laugh, comparing the two, but I couldn't help it. The sheep reminded me of our sheep and my father and me herding them on our ranch when I was a teenager.

Here is how it would go: My dad would line himself up on one side of the field on his four-wheeler. He'd put the dog in the middle and me on the other side of the field. My little brother, Dylan, who was about three at the time, would follow behind me. It wasn't like the sheep were going to trample him. They stayed as far away from us as possible.

The four of us would then attempt to maneuver the sheep to a fenced-in area on the other side of the field. The goal was to get the lambs inside the fence so we could cut their tails and testicles off. It sounds like the worst thing ever—and it was—but my dad said it had to be done. He said the tails had to be docked because they collect too many shit clods and cutting them kept flies and maggots from hanging out on crusted poo. The castration kept the male lambs from acting aggressive and getting the ewes pregnant.

Sheep are stubborn. Let me rephrase that... sheep are the most stubborn assholes ever. The more we tried to herd them, the more they'd dart away from that little fenced-in area, though I guess I didn't blame them. We'd spend hours, running and trying to corral them, while they scampered and hopped through our line.

There are few things I hate more than herding sheep. I would inevitably run past one sheep then slip in the mud, trying to chase another. Sitting in the mud, huffing and puffing one day with tears in my eyes, my dad sat on his four-wheeler, giggling at me.

"Honey, you're just trying so hard." His belly bounced with laughter.

"It's not funny. I hate this!" Miraculously, we always got the sheep into the castration area, where my father would then bite the lambs' testicles off with his teeth. He'd get on his knees, slam the lamb sideways on the ground, and bite the scrotum off. By then, Dylan was always onto something else so no, he wasn't traumatized at three by the castration-by-mouth process. As for me, I'm not sure the process traumatized me, but it definitely frightened me.

"It heals better that way. Really!" my dad would say with blood on his face.

It's actually really hard for one person to get a fighting lamb to the ground and successfully cut testicles with only two hands. That's where the teeth thing originated. It sounds weird, but us hillbillies have been doing it that way for years. Google it. I swear. I had to hold the other sheep back from the gate, so I couldn't help my dad pin the lambs down. Using his teeth was simply a gross solution to a difficult procedure.

My father sliced the tails off next. Blood shot out the holes in a straight line after the tails came off. Then the lamb would prance around, screaming in misery. Their pain and the crusted blood on my pants brought tears to my eyes again. I couldn't believe I used to help with that, but I guess I didn't have a choice.

If you didn't grow up amidst farm animals, vineyards, and numerous hunting and fishing excursions, it might be hard to understand a man like Michael Kennedy. He was an outdoorsman to the core. He built a lake in his backyard and put catfish in it so we could teach my little brother how to fish. He ate everything he killed and cared about preserving nature. He was as rugged as they came, and although his behavior scared me at times, at least I knew what to expect.

My father was pure country, which I guess added to his charm.

CHAPTER 5

Myles

WE FOUND OUR hotel in Galway, off an intimate street amidst charming houses with flower boxes perched underneath shuttered windows. The hotel was set above a pub we had to schlepp through to check in. We carried our bags between tables where old men gabbed and sipped pints of murky beer. Soft music played as a bartender meticulously wiped the counter top with a towel.

"You gals checking in?" he asked.

We stopped and looked up, surprised.

"Yeah. Hi." I waved. "Do we do it here?"

The bartender smiled. "Yeah. We're a small operation. This is sort of the front desk." The guy was handsome, with a short beard and reddish hair.

I would have flirted with him if I hadn't been so tired from the bus ride.

He gave us a large, gold key straight from 1860 and we went upstairs to take a nap. Our room looked prepped for a tea party. White ruffles with pink and purple flowers adorned the outline of the mattresses, windows, and lamp-shades. All we needed were teacups and derby hats.

Clanking glasses and light music from the pub below didn't keep us from sleeping for several hours. When Shannon and I woke, we headed out to get some grub and explore the main street where hundreds of people scampered about with shopping bags and sometimes children in their arms. Those main blocks were beyond foggy and crowded and reminded us a bit of Fishermen's Wharf in San Francisco.

Despite the bustling retail scene, Galway moved at a slower pace than Dublin. The landscape was more rural and hilly. The fog rolled over cobble-stone streets where locals gabbed and frequented pubs. Galway was easier to explore than Dublin, with less humans and a chilled-out vibe.

I bought the obligatory Irish knot jewelry for my mother and little sister, Erika. We wandered around in the murk before stopping for Beamish Stout and chips, the equivalent to our French fries. We asked some locals where the best pubs were and set out to find them using a crumpled-up map I'd been carrying around in the rain.

A few wrong turns later, we found The Crane. Packed and stuffy, the bar had a friendly vibe. People crammed onto stools and sofas placed too close to-gether. There was something comforting about it, though. The patrons at The Crane seemed to genuinely care about the people across from them. No one monitored the room to see what else was going on, like in San Francisco. In this room, everyone was totally present with the people in front of them, a state of being I longed to master.

"Hi! I'm Ginny. From America, are ya?" a rosy-faced bartender asked.

Even though I envisioned us as natural looking and inconspicuous, one way or another, people always knew we were Americans. We didn't have to say a word. "Yes. How are you?"

"I'm great. Just wanted to say hello cooz I didn't recognize ya."

Just as I'd suspected, everyone knew everyone there and they all sensed we were new. We bought beers and shot the shit with Ginny for a while until something wonderful happened.

Just about everyone in the bar—about twenty of them—unloaded instru-ments out of cases by their feet. There were young people and old... you name it. One by one, they tuned their violins, flutes, piccolos, and guitars and started playing traditional Irish Trad together. One person played first and the others followed. When a musician stopped to take a rest, it didn't matter because the other two violinists filled the empty space. The players tapped their feet and bobbed their heads, creating the kinds of melodies you hear in movies. Everybody smiled and carried on like we were all in a dream. I'd never seen anything like it.

We listened for an hour, taking pictures and letting the music and the energy in the room soak in. Some of the images turned out orangey, with arms and fingers blurring into guitar strings. I cherish those photographs. They captured all the beauty of that night.

We eventually left The Crane and headed for another bar down the street. Shannon and I followed a group of backpackers up some stairs, ending on an open roof deck. Dozens of people, bundled in down coats, gathered there under the cloudy sky to smoke cigarettes and tell stories. Intricate white Christmas lights, wrapped around wooden slats above, lit the roof like stars. We grabbed the two open stools left and sat down next to Rian and Bradley, two welcoming Irishmen who greeted us with warm smiles.

Our new friends told us how excited they were to graduate college. We hoped they were talking about something that had happened years prior. No such luck. We didn't talk about age, but it occurred to me, as Rian and Bradley spoke, that we were likely more than a decade older than them.

Rian's blond, curly hair rested on his shoulders. His blue eyes complemented a timid smile. The earthy type—sans loud voice and broad shoulders—pulled me in on occasion and Rian fit the mold. Despite his obvious shyness, I got him talking and he told me he played in a band. He looked like a guitar belonged in his arms, for sure.

Rian and Bradley invited us over to their house, and when I found out they were into video games, I got a little spring in my step. They didn't live far and we felt safe about our visit.

The house was larger than I thought it would be. It looked like something an entire family would live in, complete with a full dining room, kitchen, and several bedrooms. Rian and I played a wrestling video game in the family room and screamed at the television and each other like we were twelve.

"Yeah, sucka! That's what I thought," I boasted after winning a match.

"Oh, because you joost pushed the buttons real fast, did ya?"

"Don't try to make excuses for my skills, Rian." I laughed. Video games were my weakness. I liked them more than chocolate and needed to stay away from them. If I didn't, I could become one of those unmarried thirty-somethings sitting in my living room, addicted to Grand Theft Auto, Part 11.

When we tired of wrestling, Rian took me up to his room to show me his guitar. I realize how that sounds, but he really did just show me his guitar.

Piles of clothes covered the floor in his cave. A rusted bike leaned against a desk full of papers. Posters of musicians covered the walls and it all reminded me of high school. Despite my surroundings, I felt comfortable.

Rian's soft-spoken sweetness put me at ease and I loved being around him. He emanated kind energy, until he pulled out a knife and threatened to cut my finger off. I kid. Honestly, he was the sweetest. I lay down on the bed next to him to finally hear his skills.

Rian strummed the strings of his guitar and I floated up in the air. For me, listening to the guitar is like hearing a lullaby. It's one of my favorite things to do. It ignites tranquility inside me, often putting me to sleep.

"Hey, do you know any songs from *Once*?" he asked.

I couldn't believe it. The small Irish film was one of my favorites. It was about two people torn between old love and new love. The music in it melted my heart. The ballads were heart-wrenching tunes about loss and the pain we inflict on each other and ourselves. I listened to the songs over and over when I broke up with my boyfriend, Myles. I'd loved that guy more than the air I breathed. Sometimes, I imagined those songs had been written just for us.

Swimming in a pool of self-pity, I used to sing the lyrics with tears in my eyes. "Part of me has died and won't return. Part of me wants to hide. The part that's burned."

Now here I was, a zillion miles from Myles, and this Irish kid was asking about it. I hadn't gone back to that place for so long, but I suddenly wanted to sing every song with my new friend. I ached to swim in the memory of Myles and I knew I could, if I heard that music.

Rian picked his guitar back up and went right into one of the good ones.

"I think it's time, we give it up, and figure out, what's stopping us, from breathing easy, and talking straight..."

ℭ

Myles and I met on New Year's Eve, around my thirtieth birthday. Convinced I knew it all, I figured I would most definitely find the man of my dreams that year. I'd just moved to San Francisco and landed a great job, reporting and anchoring at a popular television station. I was making three times the amount of money I'd made at the previous station and my mother and sister, who lived nearby, could watch me on television every night.

I ran several miles from my apartment to the Golden Gate Bridge almost every day and the bay always brought a smile to my face. The city captivated me from the second I arrived. I had always yearned to be a part of the fresh salty air, towering buildings, the bay, and the romance surrounding the neighborhoods and windy streets of San Francisco. Finally, I *was*.

I mapped out my favorite blocks to run and created my own obstacle course. I'd run down one street, up a steep one, and then up some stairs into a little park. I'd do push-ups on a bench then race down another flight of stairs. When I got to those stairs, I'd always stop to take in the view.

The bridge gleamed redder every day. On my side of town, the fog lifted around noon, leaving room for a sunset of pinks and purples, mixed with seagulls and crashing waves. Yep, the world was mine the day I met him... or so I thought.

New Year's Eve is a big party in San Francisco. Some downtown streets are closed off so revelers can frolic around and spill beer on each other. I wore the perfect little black dress and felt great about myself that night. I believed I would meet someone special.

I caught up with a group of friends at a bar called Irish Bank. I had never been there and had to weave my way through masses of people to get through the front door. After I found my friends, one of them put a glittery hat on my head. I grabbed a beer and we danced to a Guns N' Roses song. That's when I bumped into a guy named, Paul.

Paul and I chatted for about a minute before I detected a wedding ring on his finger. I asked if he had any cute, single friends and he pointed to a smiling guy nearby. Myles, laughed and danced with his arms in the air. He looked like a monkey, pulling his feet up in a march to the music. He was silly and adorable. I tilted my head and smirked, watching him. I may have fallen in love with Myles before I even heard his voice.

"Myles, this is Michelle," Paul yelled over the music.

"I like your hat!" He pointed at my hat.

"Thanks. It's my lucky hat."

Awkward.

"Want to keep dancing?" he asked.

"Sure."

We danced and asked each other questions. The interviewing came naturally to both of us since I was a reporter and he worked in law enforcement. Dancing questions are the best, too, because I had to bury my mouth in his neck to be heard over the music. This presented an excellent opportunity for sniffing and intimate lip-to-ear contact.

"I chased some criminals over a fence the other day, but I lost them."

"Oh, yeah? Well I just did a live interview with Mayor Newsom." I'd gotten really nervous and flubbed the beginning of that live shot (due to the perfection of Newsom's face), but I wasn't ready to reveal my fallibility yet.

Our exchange was a bit of an ego fest, for sure; I guess most first meetings are. *Listen to how smart I am. Let me tell you how great of a job I have.*

Those first encounters are so lame because people rarely ask the important stuff. I think we should ask each other different questions, like what makes a person happy and what their best friend would say about them. Who is their favorite person and what do they look forward to the most? These questions may sound corny, but they tell so much more about someone than where they work.

I brushed my lips across his ear; inhaling him was like ingesting an elixir. He smelled like April freshness and I loved it. Something about Myles filled my stomach so full of butterflies; I thought I might flutter out the window. I liked his hazel eyes, jet-black hair, and short beard. He had a little Don Draper thing going on, but more bohemian. I liked that he was much taller than me and had sparkling white teeth. I liked that I wanted to kiss him really, really badly.

After we danced and talked for a while, I suggested we go get something to eat to get our first date out of the way. "Then we don't have to pick out an outfit. It cuts down on all that nervous anticipation."

Myles thought that was about the best idea he'd ever heard, so we walked to a cute Italian place on Columbus in North Beach. As soon as our butts hit the seats, a server brought us a basket of bread with a bowl of garlic and oil.

"If we eat that, we'll be all garlicky when we kiss," Myles said.

I leaned in about five inches from his face. "We wouldn't want that to happen."

He moved forward, filled the gap and kissed me. I spun. That kiss was so good, in fact, I decided then that I would marry him. I just knew he was my guy. In my head, I was already telling the story to our kids. I wish I could go back to that night, hit myself over the head with a stale loaf of sourdough, and tell myself to be more practical. I wouldn't have listened to me, though.

The waiter saw us kissing and playfully yelled across the room. "Heya! Stop that! This is a fam-ah-lee restaurant!"

We blushed and fell deeper into love soup.

For the next couple of months, my feet didn't hit the ground. Nothing could take the smile off my face. Myles was so different compared to everyone else... or so I thought. He truly was the most interesting man I'd ever met.

Myles played with my hair. He texted me all day and made me laugh. He sent me flowers and got me personalized stationery with my name painted on the front. He asked me, "Who's pretty? You!" He hugged me and made me salads. He put ice on my knee when I fell and played guitar for me when I took a bath. The guitar playing made me feel safe because he played it to calm me down. That's why it was still so soothing for me to hear.

My love was wicked smart, but strange. Sometimes, I'd come to his house and he'd stand in the corner and say he was scared of me. I thought he was trying to be funny. Now, I believe he was trying to tell me early on about his commitment issues, but I didn't want to listen.

He frequently shot down my ideas and corrected my grammar. I, in turn, screamed at him and threw things to get his attention.

"Why don't you ever plan anything?"

"Stop trying to be my mother!"

"You need counseling!"

"You're the one who needs counseling!"

Within a matter of weeks, our relationship became an unhealthy battleground. Each of us fought to be right, not to be nice. Instead, Myles and I hit and pounded each other's hearts with our words.

I will show you I can hurt you more. That was our game and we played it to perfection.

On the other hand, the good times in between were amazing and that's what kept me from leaving him. The sex was incredible and we rolled around day and night those first couple months. When it wasn't incredible, we blamed each other and launched into more fights.

I tried to overlook our chaos and focus on how I melted when he entered a room. Life would stop and I would find myself facing the man who made my heart skip. I feel that skip even now. I loved him in a crazy way and I thought if I lost his love, I might actually die. Our love, however, was like the clearest, most rejuvenating water mixed with scalding flames. We were either screaming at each other or having sex. We were so extreme, we never found a middle ground.

He was my distraction though. He kept me from dealing with the void created by my dad's death. Our intensity occupied the best and worst parts of me, while our highs and lows mimicked interactions with my father. My relationship with Myles was so obsessive, it didn't give me time to focus on other pain.

"Sooooo, I guess you want to get married then?" Myles asked me this on his birthday, a few months into the relationship.

I'll never forget it. We were at a bar in Big Sur, overlooking cliffs that cascaded into the beautiful Pacific Ocean below. I swung my arms around his neck and almost fell off my stool. "Are you kidding? Yes!" In my delusion, I thought his question was a version of a proposal.

He awkwardly sipped his beer as I squeezed him. Like a hummingbird, his words then hovered around us and hauled ass out the window, never to be heard again.

We never made an actual plan; it was more like a hypothetical question. I wasn't afraid to talk about marriage after that, but each time the word escaped my lips, he backed farther and farther away. Myles put it on the table, but I knew he wished he hadn't.

In the interest of full disclosure, I was a total handful in that relationship. I'd made Myles my entire life and only wanted to spend time with him. I'm sure the pressure to keep me entertained hadn't been easy to deal with. I'd practically moved into his apartment. Looking back, I wish I had created more of a life for myself. Instead, I glommed onto him like a leech and rarely gave him any space. I also could have walked away when the fights intensified, but I screamed back and willingly remained fifty percent of our mess.

A turning point happened when Myles and I were on a run along the Embarcadero in San Francisco, about six months into the relationship. I'd questioned whether or not he wanted to have kids with me and he magnified my insecurity when he asked, "What if you were married and your husband changed his mind about wanting kids. What would you do?"

Annoyed and frustrated, I stopped running. "I'd divorce him. I would be completely bummed out and sad, so he probably wouldn't be happy with me anymore anyway."

"You don't even know the reason."

"Well, if there was a legitimate reason, like he or I found out we were infertile, that would be different."

"That's not what you said, though. You would just divorce him. That's just great!"

"Are you talking about yourself?"

"No. It's a hypothetical question, Michelle! Don't you understand what that is?"

"Yes, Myles. I just find it hard to believe it's not about you. Nevertheless, if he changed his mind for no reason, I would be really hurt, especially if we'd envisioned raising a family together. Not if there was a reason, though."

"That isn't what you said!"

"Yes, it is, Myles."

"No, it isn't. I can't believe you would just leave someone if they became paralyzed and couldn't have children anymore." Myles was fully healthy and fertile, by the way.

"What the hell are you even talking about?"

Plug this conversation into about fifty different scenarios and that was our relationship. Myles would throw these hypothetical questions out there—that covertly related to him, most of the time—I would answer wrong, and he would hate me for several days afterward. I lost the hypothetical game every time, which was the point. I can't understand why he didn't just break up with me. It felt like he didn't fully want me, but he didn't want to lose me, either.

We rode our roller coaster for about a year. Once a week, I'd grab all the things I kept at his apartment—toothbrush, face wash, some clothes, my guitar—and make dramatic exits. Then, he'd show up at my door, all adorable, and we'd press replay on our routine, over and over. I fake broke up with him often. Usually, the break ups lasted an hour or two. Sometimes, they'd last for weeks.

When Myles got approved for a job transfer to another country, I didn't know what to do because I'd broken up with him the night before.

"You were supposed to go with me. Now what are we going to do?"

The transfer was for a three-year stint. I didn't want to move, but the thought of him leaving devastated me. Over the course of our relationship, Myles applied to relocate to several different countries and we loved talking about how much fun we'd have in each place. Now that the transfer had gone through, I wondered if I thirsted for him or the adventure.

Despite our recent breakup, we discussed the possibility of reuniting and starting again. We agreed to think it through while he trained in another state for the new assignment. I didn't have a key to his place anymore, so I'd sometimes enter the code and sneak into his garage to feel close to him. I'd get gussied up to anchor the news then go and stand in his garage like a drone. I can see myself, crying in my suit next to his motorcycle and a pile of trash. I don't think I had one shred of self-esteem left, at that point.

Myles came home from the training a month later and I leapt back into his arms and his bed like he was oxygen to keep me alive. He said he would find an apartment in his new city, while I organized my life in preparation for the move. He said he wanted to make sure I would like it there first. I can't believe I considered dropping my job and graduate school for the relationship. He was my addiction and I couldn't let go.

I struggled to reach him after he left. The conversations were short and he always seemed to be at or on his way to a party. I knew something was amiss. He was so far away from me; I had no way of knowing if he'd found someone else. About three weeks after he left, I called him and told him I couldn't do it. I couldn't be in a relationship like this and I couldn't move with him.

"But I love you and I picked out an apartment you will really like. I got the one with the pool, just for you."

"Then why haven't I heard from you for a week? What exactly is the plan?"

"I've been super busy and I had to buy plane tickets for my parents to come out at Christmas."

"Am I coming out at Christmas?" *Silence.* "I don't get where I fit into all of this, Myles. You won't tell me." *More silence.* "I can't do this. I just don't get what's going on." I wouldn't have admitted it then, but the only way I could get his attention was to remove myself and see if he'd come and get me.

My plan worked. About a week later, Myles flew back to San Francisco. I just knew he was ready to commit, but the fairytale I had in mind ended when he told me he'd spent some time with two other women.

He cried and told me he'd messed up. He also said the experience made him realize he was finally ready for marriage. "I got it all out of my system, Michelle. I'm ready to go."

Lucky me.

"I thought you were looking for apartments that would be good for both of us? This is so mean."

"I know. I'm sorry. I freaked out."

I almost threw up that night, standing at the sink, sobbing, and trying to catch my breath. Devastated, I knew for the sake of dignity alone, I could never be with him again. I didn't trust him and our situation made me feel terrible about myself. Although, by staying in the relationship in the first place, I'd clearly never felt good about myself to begin with. On top of that, at the time, the status of our relationship was incredibly vague. We hadn't established whether we were 100% together in a long time, so technically, he was free to do whatever he wanted. Despite the circumstances, the thought of our relationship ending for good, crushed me.

He wanted to have sex that night just as much as I did, but I couldn't. It's weird to want to be close to someone you hate and love at the same time. The thought of him with someone else after being there a month sent me dry-heaving back to the sink. We talked all night, but mostly dragged out a long-overdue farewell.

When I dropped him off at the airport the next day, he hugged me and said it would be all right. I still hoped, but I knew it would never work. Saying goodbye felt like death. I grabbed on tight and buried my face in his skin one last time. I smelled him through my tears then jumped up into his arms and he held me, my legs dangling down like a child's. He wasn't coming back. I would never smell or see him again.

When he got into the terminal, he texted me that he'd seen the "truth in my eyes." To this day, I'm not sure what that meant. We'd said goodbye, but I figured we'd speak again. We emailed a little, but surprisingly, we really never spoke to each other again.

I loved Myles more than I can ever explain on these pages. If I could rest my head in his neck right now and kiss his face, I would... just for a moment. It would be hard not to crumble into his arms like I used to. Even in another country, I let him haunt me for months.

The breakup broke my heart in ways I didn't know were possible. I dreamt about him. I could still see him dancing that first night. Because sorrow sinks and swells into the same abyss, losing Myles also forced me to resume treading the water of my dad's passing. Our separation created space for me to think about the other grief I didn't want to face.

In the months that followed, I went on dates, wishing every guy was Myles, or my version of what I wanted Myles to be. About a month after he left, my addiction emailed, saying he was close to making a huge "gesture" and wanted to come home to me for good. Then he wrote back and said he was afraid. Around that time, I drunk dialed his cell phone and sang a Norah Jones song into his voicemail. I then called back and left ANOTHER message singing a Beatles' song. I woke up the next morning, thinking I might die of embarrassment. We never spoke of it. Maybe it wasn't his number anymore and someone else had gotten it.

I hope.

It's been a year since Myles and I emailed. I have no idea where he is or what he's doing. Even though I'm embarrassed to admit it, our breakup still hurts. I believe that him getting that job was divine intervention, but I can't scratch him out of my head. I know he's not the right person for me and I can never be with him, but logic and understanding what is right don't erase the wanting.

Sometimes, in my dreams, Myles and my father's faces mix together, like a face that resembles both of them. The loss of the two biggest men in my life bleeds together into one excruciating wound. I have to heal the wound and move on.

I'm trying.

♃

Rian sang his heart out that night as I lay on the bed next to him. His head stretched back as he crooned the words I equally loved and hated. The next thing I knew, I was singing too, and we didn't sound half bad together. We wailed like we were on stage, despite the fact that it was three in the morning. I remembered every lyric and every tear I cried for Myles. The music took me right back. In those moments, I also remembered the pain, but discerned how much things had changed. I let the memories swim in, but I didn't cry. I missed Myles, but loved singing songs with my new, very young, Irish, guitar-playing companion.

Rian hummed with his eyes closed and I felt calm. I was in my moment, not Myles's. He had left and I survived. *I'm getting better.* I smiled and stared at the Social Distortion poster on the ceiling.

Rian stopped singing. "Have ya ever loved that hard?" He must have seen it all over my face.

"Yes, and my heart broke beyond anything I can explain to you."

"Try. I want to know."

"His name was Myles. We fought all the time. I acted crazy with him, but I also loved him more than anyone. Believe me, heartbreak is up there with experiencing death."

"You wouldn't take it back though, would ya?"

"The breakup? Yes. One hundred percent. That experience was horrible."

"No, the time ya had with him."

I didn't know it until I found his band playing on a YouTube page that Rian was indeed twenty-three years old. He was a decade behind me after all. What a question. What a point.

"No, never, ever, ever. I loved him like he was a part of my body."

I would have gone through it all again—to make love, to dance with him, to watch him goof off to make me laugh. To hear him laugh, I would do it all again. I couldn't believe I said it, but I would take those bullets to experience the joy that came with them; like bleeding with a smile on my face.

"I want that," he said. "I want the love and the pain."

"You really want to feel that pain?"

"Yeah, I want to feel the real thing."

Rian and I sang and played guitar until the sun came up. We never kissed and I'm not sure I wanted to. Don't get me wrong, he was sweet, with his tender smile and curls like mine. Sometimes he'd touch my cheek with the back of his hand and it felt good. It was nice to hang with someone so gentle. I didn't need anything else.

Actually, yes, I did. I always did… just not from Rian.

CHAPTER 6

— ✿ —

Fight or Flight

CONTENT WITH GALWAY, we headed up to the North Ireland capital of Belfast. The city is so rich in history, we couldn't explore it without bumping into a building that had survived twenty bombings or a wall still separating a Catholic neighborhood from a Protestant one. The largest city in Northern Ireland, Belfast, had a little of everything including a harbor, towering buildings, castles, and grassy knolls leading up to Parliament and a robust city hall.

Murals of the IRA with their guns drawn were prominently displayed throughout the industrial city. The people in Belfast say they want the murals taken down, but no one ever does it. The police stations were still covered with huge barricades of bulletproof glass. To us, the conflicts—or "troubled times"—happened eons ago. To the people living in Belfast, the fighting that took place from the 1970s through the 1990s happened yesterday.

I should preface my description of "our" battle in Belfast by saying that the week leading up to getting there was stressful for both of us. I was surprised to discover that the exact highs and lows I'd experienced back home, followed me on the road. Shannon and I thought the trip of a lifetime should feel wonderful all of the time, but it didn't. I wanted to be glad I didn't have any responsibilities, but instead, I felt like I had no control over my life and my feet weren't planted on the ground.

I felt blessed to be traveling and ungrateful for feeling lonely. I checked my email in hopes that someone would write and tell me they miss me… someone other than my mother and best friend, Jessica. I wanted a solution to appear, but it never did. Self-pity followed me around like a co-dependent kitten.

In Belfast, I read Tom Robbins's *Still Life with Woodpecker*. In the book, Robbins asks if anyone knows how to make love stay. That question resonated with me for days. I'd never succeeded at making love stay and even though I didn't have a boyfriend, I worried that when I did find love again, I wouldn't be able to make it stay. *Nothing is permanent, Michelle. I know, but that doesn't mean I don't get sad about it.* I guess I just had to accept I couldn't keep anything forever. Love is a tumbleweed; eventually, the wind or life takes it to another place. It's heartbreaking for me to think of love that way. I want to know I can hold love in my hand and have no fear of it leaving, but I can't, and I end up grieving before it even starts.

Tired and irritable, Shannon and I went out for drinks to unwind. We watched a band play and ended up hanging out with hot blond Aaron, from Belfast, and black-haired Randal, from London. By the time we got to their hotel lobby for a nightcap, it was around two in the morning. The two of us didn't know at the time that the Europa Hotel we were sitting in had been bombed twenty-eight times back in the nineties.

In a conversation with Randal, Shannon said that the worldly perception of Americans is that we are loud and obnoxious. She also said the perception is correct.

The statement angered me and in my need to defend my people, I told her she shouldn't say that. "Shannon, not all Americans are loud and obnoxious."

"That's not what I said. I said the perception is that Americans are loud and obnoxious. I know, I lived in London."

That statement kicked off a new war in the North. When I visualize the two of us, screaming at each other in that hotel bar, it makes me laugh now.

"What's your problem?"

"You are the loud and obnoxious one."

"No, you are."

"Get out of my face!"

"You are the rudest person I've ever met!"

Essentially, we proved that Americans are, indeed, loud and obnoxious. Shannon ended up storming out and I followed, because she had the only key to our room. Those guys must have thought we were nuts.

Back at the hotel, we screamed at each other with venom. We used all the good swear words and took out every last bit of fear and anxiety we had, on each other.

"You're a total bitch."

"You're a know it all."

"You're the moodiest person ever."

"Fine. Maybe we aren't compatible."

"I don't need you to travel."

"Whatever. I don't, either."

And there it was... the possibility of us splitting up.

We knew the fight had nothing to do with Americans and everything to do with both of us feeling out of sorts... not grounded. We loved traveling more than anything, but we had gone from a structured lifestyle to anything-goesville. For two people with colossal control issues, the transition had proven difficult.

We went to bed feeling awful and tossed and turned a lot that night. We worried about stumbling so soon, with months left to go on our journey. After waking up, we apologized and agreed to spend the day apart. We decided to come back together after we'd had time to think and cool off.

I called my mother and, like always, she dropped everything to listen to me. Loyal as ever, she'd always tell me if she thought I was wrong about something.

Heavy raindrops pounded the phone booth walls as I cried to her. "I don't know, Mom. This is all so anxiety-ridden. Sometimes we look around and it's way scarier than I thought it would be. If we fight, then who can we count on besides ourselves? I mean, I can rely on myself, but I need her here. I just feel alone."

"I know you're sad, sweetie, but most likely, Shannon is feeling as bad as you are right now and she's probably talking to her mom, too. Do you want to go out on your own?"

I thought about it. Could I handle it on my own? I definitely could and my angry side—ego—wanted to show Shannon she couldn't treat me that way. I could take myself away from her, but the thought of it seemed immature. I wasn't surprised by my instincts; my flight response developed in childhood. Growing up in chaotic environments, I'd perfected fight or flight to art-form-status.

I lived with my mother, my older brother, Ryan, and my stepfather, in the San Francisco Bay Area, from the time I was six until I was sixteen. My stepfather wasn't the kindest person toward my brother and me, and communication in that household involved a fair amount of yelling. When I was younger, I was too afraid to leave, but when my mom decided to divorce him, I seized the opportunity to move, as well, to see what it would be like to live with my father full-time. So, at sixteen, while my mother struggled through her second divorce, I moved from her house in the city to my father's ranch in Lodi. My older brother, Ryan, had moved there a year before that, so both of us lived with my dad from age sixteen to eighteen, before we went away to college. My dad had never experienced raising two teenagers, so we all fought... a lot.

When I argued with my father about curfews, grades, and boys, I had the urge to flit back over to my mom's again, but I didn't. I figured I needed to stop running for once and I committed to staying there for the next couple of years. I was used to either fighting for my life or running for my life. I'd never known much of a middle ground, so staying to work things out and communicating like an adult, had never come easy. Shannon had also lived through some divorce growing up, so she was coming from a similar place.

Speaking with my mother, I thought about how much fun Shannon and I had together. We loved nothing more than gallivanting around, goofing off, and making each other laugh. We could go off alone, but I didn't want to. My friendship with Shannon motivated me to stay and deal with our feud. I knew the practice of facing the situation, rather than running from it, would help me in future relationships. I thanked my mother and told her I wouldn't quit. She told me she missed me and I told her I missed her back.

Soaking wet, I opened our hotel room door to find Shannon, downcast and lying on the bed. "Shannon, I don't want to fight with you and I don't want to quit. You're all I have out here so if we fight, I feel really alone."

"I know. I agree. It's just stressful and all the moving around and packing and unpacking doesn't help. It's hard for me, too."

"I think we should promise to never do that again. No swearing at each other. And if we get mad and want to kill each other, we just have to say, 'I'm pissed and need a break and let's talk about this in a bit'."

"You don't want to separate, right?" Shannon asked.

"No. I am trying to not take the easy way out. I don't want to run from you."

"I don't want to run, either." We sat on the edge of our beds, nodding in awkward silence.

"I bought us some socks." I said.

Tension broken.

"Oh! Me needs," Shannon squeaked.

And with that, I pulled out the new socks I had bought on that day-o-sucki-ness. I gave Shannon the pink ones and kept the blue ones for myself. We slipped them on and lay down next to each other with our legs shooting straight up in the air. With pointed toes, we got back to normal.

Shannon bent her toes toward her foot like a mouth talking. "Oh, hello, Mr. Blue Sock. How are you?"

"Ohhhh, hello, Mr. Pink Sock. Would you like to go and get some pizza for dinner?" my foot replied.

"Why, yes. I have never tasted pizza before. That sounds dee-lish-oussss."

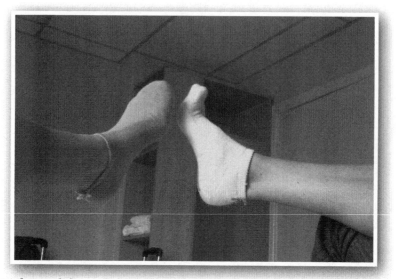

We learned from that experience. I never, ever wanted to go through a fight and separation like that again and Shannon didn't, either. We fought again, but it never looked as ugly and we treated each other with more kindness and respect after that.

CHAPTER 7

— ✿ —

With or Without You

SHANNON AND I landed in Edinburgh, on the southern half of Scotland, and fell in love with the landscape. Stony buildings lined the streets like miniature Hogwarts. A massive castle sat high on a hilltop in the middle of the city. When we got there, Shannon took a nap and I took a jog to go see the castle up close. I didn't last long running due to "out-of-shape-ness," so I speed-walked through streets full of people and walls made of granite. The castle looked awesome up close.

Sprawling parks also stretch across Edinburgh, many of which are private. The parks are actually enclosed in fences and you need a key to get in. I strolled past several of them, trying the gate locks without success. I wondered why a park needed to be private. Then, I rounded a corner onto a street right out of a fairytale.

On Edinburgh's most popular street, the Miracle Mile, performers frolicked in front of massive cathedrals. Choir groups sang on stages as jugglers and musicians weaved their art through crowds of clapping people. A clown on stilts played an accordion right above my head. Absorbing it all, each sound colliding with the next, I remembered Edinburgh's famous music and arts festival had kicked off that week. *What great timing!*

I stopped to listen to an all-men's choir belt out some of the tunes from *Rent*. I liked the music so much, I ordered a turkey sandwich nearby so I could sit and keep listening. That particular street reminded me of a *Robin Hood* movie or a renaissance fair, but a thousand times better. Dozens of artists and actors pranced by, wearing dresses from long ago. People performed magic acts amidst singers, switching off on different stages along the street. I could have stayed there forever, just watching.

I wandered around The Elephant House Cafe where J.K. Rowling apparently wrote her first *Harry Potter* book. I sat down and wrote a little, hoping to be inspired. I wondered how Rowling had come up with such incredible fiction when I struggled to write stories that had actually happened.

That night, Shannon and I went out to explore some local bars. We ended up at a steamy, packed pub where another group of young men celebrated a stag party. They pounced as I stood at the bar, ordering a drink.

A tall guy wearing a pink sweater approached first. "Is your name Barbara?"

"No, sorry."

"Oh, because we're trying to find a gal named Barbara for our friend to kiss. It's his stag party and we have a list of things he has to do."

I wasn't a Barbara, but we ended up talking to the group of about seven guys for a while anyway.

The one getting hitched told me he was afraid to be with the same person forever. "I mean, I'm so young. I'm twenty-six. I'm a little freaked out."

I tried not to laugh. Oh, twenty-six. How far away it seemed to me standing there. "Well, are you sure this is the right girl?"

"Yes! She's great. I mean, she would kill me if she knew I was standing here, talking to girls like this."

"What do you mean? Girls in general? It's your bachelor party and you're at a bar. Of course you're going to talk to girls."

"She just gets jealous."

"You aren't doing anything wrong."

"Well, I would like to kiss you."

"Are you sure you want to be married?"

"Yes, I guess. I just feel like how should I know if this is the right one?" The fears he contemplated probably should have been addressed long before the stag party, but what did I know? I didn't know him; I just knew his concerns weren't far off from lots of people's. Whether you are a man or a woman, young or old, it's scary to commit forever. Maybe I'd feared commitment like Myles had, but couldn't admit that to myself at the time. Sometimes, I think we get so busy chasing in a relationship, we lose sight of our own fears and "forever" issues.

"How old are ya, anyway?" he asked.

And there it was. I wondered what reaction I'd get this time. "I'm thirty-three."

He looked at me as if I was already connected to life support. "That's really old, Michelle."

"Yeah. Good thing you didn't have to kiss me. My dentures might have fallen out in your mouth."

He looked disgusted.

I smiled, curtsied, and walked away.

I used to worry about thirty. I was afraid people would look at me and wonder, "What's wrong with her? Why isn't she married yet?" The thing is, I'm more comfortable with myself now than I've ever been. I feel good in my skin, even though the stitches in my jeans are struggling to break free from my expanding ass cheeks. I get scared, but I'm strong. I'm doing everything I said I would, and I'm glad I haven't gotten married yet. *Am I telling the truth right now, or am I terrified?*

I wish I were twenty-six again. *That's the truth.* I worry I won't find the right guy and have babies before my insides turn to shrubbery. *More truth.* I wish I looked better naked. *Keep going.* Sometimes I love myself and sometimes I can't stand myself. When I chase after unavailable men, I can't stand myself. When I avoid relationships—even though being in one is the best thing ever—because I'm scared of breaking up, I can't stand myself. I wish I weren't so afraid of divorce. I can't help it.

∝♭

I'm seven years old, on the phone with my father. My mother is standing over me, yelling at him through the receiver. I'm the go-between as each parent fires messages through me.

"You tell him that I will not drive you. If he wants to see you, he should come and pick you guys up himself!"

"Oh, yeah? Well your mother shouldn't have moved to the goddamn Bay Area! If I have to come and get you, she should bring you back, goddammit! We need to share the driving!" *The phone is now a stick of dynamite in my hand.*

"No! I won't do it!"

"Fine!" He slams the receiver down and hangs up. I hold the phone, wishing my dad would come back on so I can ask him about his fishing trip.

My mother stomps away and I'm left standing there. I'm an inch tall.

"Well, does that mean we aren't going?" I ask the air.

My parents got married a couple years after high school and divorced eight years later, when I was two. After their divorce, my older brother, Ryan, and I moved with my mother back to the house where she grew up in Lodi.

Kids dominated the quaint country neighborhood and we enjoyed our nights playing in the street. We came in when my mother yelled out into the darkness that it was time. Ryan and I didn't worry about a thing and we loved living there. My twenty-eight-year-old mom, on the other hand, struggled to pay rent and raise two kids alone. Those days could not have been easy for her. She was several years younger than I am now, doing it by herself.

When she met my soon-to-be stepfather, my mother fell in love and jumped at the chance for a new happiness. Unfortunately, he lived about an hour and a half away and my father raged about my mom moving us. The fights had already begun between my mom and dad. They intensified after we moved.

My brother and I stayed with my father in the summer and on some holidays. He hooked up with my future stepmother shortly after he and my mother broke up. I was three when they met; I think she was twenty-two.

The visits weren't as often as I would've liked, but when I did see my dad, he really did entertain my older brother and me. He used to take us to his motorcycle races where he'd whip around corners on his red and black bike. Our hero skyrocketed dirt into the air as he flew over jumps.

"Go, Dad!" we'd scream out to him. Upon crossing the finish line, my father would get off his bike and collapse in the dirt, exhausted. I'd plop down next to him, hoping he'd get up and sit me on the bike. Sometimes he did.

When I was three, he'd put me in his lap and ask, "Who's your favorite daddy?"

"Me!" I was so young, I'd always mess it up.

My dad would howl with laughter. "Who's my favorite daughter?"

"You!"

We loved that game until I got it right; then it wasn't funny anymore. I jumped into my dad's lap well into my teens. I'd curl up while he read the paper, hoping to get some attention. Sometimes, I got it and sometimes, I'd just sit there, watching him devour the business section.

After six years together, when I was about nine, my dad married my step-mother, but didn't tell us. I found out by discovering some pictures in a drawer several months later.

"But wait? Why didn't we get to come?" My voice cracked with emotion.

"It was hard enough trying to plan that thing, let alone worrying about driving two hours in traffic to get you guys," my dad said.

My feelings of worthlessness started at an early age.

Marriage should last forever. *At least it's supposed to, right?* So why rush into something that's going to last for decades? I'd rather do as much as I can before I go down that road because once kids come, everything changes. I get that.

I used to feel rushed. I used to worry about my clock ticking—I still do—but there's no way I'm going to pick someone for the sole purpose of having children. I'd rather hold out for someone I'm compatible with and adopt if I get too old... or not have children at all.

I want a strong man who knows himself. I want him to be my best friend, someone who has ambition... and my back. I will be his most enthusiastic cheerleader. We'll watch *Workaholics* and roll around naked on Sundays, and he'll like pizza as much as I do. He'll also let me love him as hard as I want and won't run when I open my heart to him. I don't feel these are impossible requests. I just have to figure out how to stay when I meet him. I have a tendency to get nervous when a guy wants to be there and isn't running from me.

Please, God, help me change that about myself.

∝

When the bar closed, the husband-to-be's friends had to hold him up and lead him out into the street. His head hung low and his feet dragged behind him.

I hope the man I end up with doesn't look like that on his bachelor party night. Hopefully, he glows and gives high fives to his friends.

Glasgow isn't a very dazzling city, but U2 picked it, so we did, too. We arrived at Hampden Park Arena early the next day and got a strange look when a security guard checked my bag and grabbed on to Tiny Elvis. The guard tilted his head and glared at me... hard. I didn't say a word, won the staring contest, and moved on. What could I say? "I love this doll and he wanted to hear U2?" I opted for silence.

We positioned ourselves only twenty feet from the stage and watched some smaller bands play before the big show. Shannon and I stood like bricks, boxing out anyone who tried to encroach on our spot. We took silly pictures of Tiny Elvis crowd surfing while we waited.

"Now look at that stage. That thing is huuuuuge!" We enjoyed Tiny Elvis, as usual. He never disappointed.

The crowd went bananas when Bono finally pranced out in that way only he can, with his pelvis out and his back arched. Praying mantis posture aside, he looked like a rocker, even after all these years. Bono sounded heavenly. His lyrics boomed and swam through me.

"In the naaaaame of love!"

We sang along at the top of our lungs.

"What more in the name of love!"

Rain fell on our heads and cooled us off. I stuck Tiny Elvis halfway down my shirt with his arms raised up to the sky, as U2 went through the classics. "With or Without You" took me back twenty-two years. I closed my eyes and saw our fishing boat.

ᑦᑬ

I'm eleven years old, listening to "With or Without You" on my Walkman. My father steers the boat through whitecaps near Point Reyes, off the Northern California Coast. He's excited for our first deep-sea fishing excursion of the season. I don't usually get queasy, but that particular day, as I listen to The Joshua Tree tape, I feel seasick.

"Go to sleep. I told you, just lie down and your stomach won't hurt anymore."

"But I want to catch some salmon."

The boat motor gurgles. "You will. I'll wake you up once we get out far enough."

The waves crest black and monstrous. Buttery clouds hang, gloomy and freezing. Shivering, I pull the sleeves of my sweater over my hands and lie down, using my dad's leg as a pillow. I drift off while my dad steers the motor through chop. Fishing poles and nets clank against the side of the boat as Bono sings, "I can't live, with or without you," in my ears.

The smell of the pancakes my stepmother packed wakes me up. I open my eyes and see my dad, bearded and laughing, waving a cold flapjack in front of my nose. I grab it and shove it in my mouth.

"This is the spot, honey. You're gonna catch a big one. I can feel it." His Coke-bottle-thick glasses are misty in the ocean air.

God, he was nerdy. God, I loved him. My dad was right, though. I caught a thirty-pound salmon that day.

ᑦᑬ

Shannon and I stayed in Glasgow overnight. We flew out to the southern tip of Portugal the next day. The flight was long, but we looked forward to seeing the beach again.

That Scotland gets cold.

CHAPTER 8

❦

Dylan

THE CRACKED CLIFFS along the western edge of Portugal reminded me of Big Sur, in California. Many of the buildings in Portugal are white and contrast beautifully with the dark blue water, splashing nearby. The people there looked a little Spanish and little Italian to me, but they prefer not to be associated with anyone else. Portuguese people are proud, and they aren't afraid to tell you to hurry up if you can't decide which ice cream flavor to order.

Our experience in Portugal started out in Cascais, a quaint town in the middle of the western coast of the country. We rolled our suitcases along several cobblestone blocks before we discovered the hotel we booked was really an old apartment, set off by itself on a secluded street. Shannon and I envisioned creepsters following us in the night and opted for a legitimate hotel down the road. That hotel had bunk beds and pink tile in a shared bathroom, but we didn't mind. Dirty hair, uneven mattresses, and communal bathrooms were getting easier to live with.

Sweltering, we dropped our stuff and took off for the water, only to find there wasn't much of a beach in Cascais. To our dismay, hordes of children played in front of us on about six square feet of sand. We turned around, saw a pub, and opted for Plan B.

Shannon and I sat on a patio, listening to a local band and admired the magenta sunset glistening behind them. Portugal wasn't so bad, after all. About five beers in, we decided a jumping contest was in order.

"Let's jump as high as we can by that fountain and use the sports photography setting on the camera to get some action shots." My beer-influenced brain was clearly hard at work.

Each of us took turns catapulting ourselves off one of the steps by the ornate fountain. Confused passers-by stopped, watching us holding poses in the air. Some laughed. Some probably thought we were crazy. The fountain lights created colorful streams as we pushed our hands to the sky. With legs bent, we smiled at the camera, posing with our hair curled around our faces. Another dumb, fun time I loved.

The next day, I waited in line for gelato behind about twenty-five people. Exploring the town, I almost tripped over the line and decided to join the crowd. I wasn't in the mood for sugar, but figured if that many people were waiting, it had to be something special.

Kids picked their noses next to moms, scrolling through their phones to pass the time in line. News articles praising the owners adorned the walls of the shop, and I just knew it would be delicious.

Finally, I made it to the front, but I balked when asked to order. Unable to translate the menu, I blurted out, "Chocolate and caramel!" A hairy man, with a face like a dried up plum, gave me a cone with two scoops. I squeezed my way back out through the twenty more people who had lined up and dug in.

A couple of bites into my treat, I realized the caramel tasted strange. I should have just ordered chocolate. With the two flavors mushed together, I either had to eat them both or throw the whole thing away. Get serious though. Who is throwing gelato out? All I could think about was how Cold Stone back home was so much better.

I wandered and ate my cone, thinking about how my friend, Laura, and I used to do ice cream drive-bys in Chico. There were never any open parking spaces in front of the Cold Stone on 2nd Street, so I would drive and she would run in and get me peanut butter and chocolate. Hers would have a gallon of marshmallow cream on top. Man, she loved that marshmallow cream. She always did a goofy dance while she waited for me to drive back around the block to pick her up. Then, she'd stick her thumb out like a hitchhiker. I missed her so much. I missed her, Cold Stone, and home, in general.

Shannon and I spent only a few days in Cascais. We didn't fall in love with the place and decided to board a train for the capital city of Lisbon. When our train stopped in Lisbon, we had our first really bad experience of the trip.

Waiting for a bus on the curb, I noticed my back felt naked. *Panic.* Patting my shoulders, I confirmed I'd left my backpack—with Tiny Elvis and my laptop inside—on the train. In my mind, I saw the backpack on a high shelf. I had placed it up above my head and forgot to grab it because the pack wasn't in my line of vision.

I ran as fast as I could to check the train, but when I got back into the station, I couldn't remember which car we had taken. The seven trains in front of me morphed into seventy. Unsure which one to inspect first, I started at the first one and scoured through them all. The pack wasn't anywhere.

Shannon went to search the trains for a second time. I waited, heart pounding, at the bus stop, with all our other bags piled around me. The loss hit me and tears followed. I felt so far away from home, and I really loved that Tiny Elvis doll. I tried not to be so attached, but I couldn't help it. My best friend had given him to me and I missed her, too.

I sobbed into my hand until a Portuguese woman waiting for the bus put her arm around me. Then, I buried my face in her shoulder, pretending she was my mom. I knew she was just trying to be there for me. I explained what had happened, but I don't think she understood a word I said. It was nice of her, though, to do her best for a stranger. She just rubbed my back and let me know I wasn't alone.

Shannon couldn't find the backpack, either, so we booked a hotel room nearby and planned to return in a few hours to check the lost and found. I checked it once, but they told me to come back later. I'd lost hope. I was also devastated and angry with myself for being so careless. I called my best friend and cried into the phone.

"I lost Tiny Elvis, Jess."

"Wait, where? What happened? Are you all right?"

"Yes. I just left my backpack on the train and I can't find it. My laptop and a whole bunch of other stuff is in there, too," I blubbered.

"Well, what are you doing sitting there? Go turn that train station upside down. Go find it!"

She was right. Crying about it didn't solve anything, so I picked myself up and took a cab back to the station. Defeated, I approached the lost and found window, which was about to close. I asked the attendant to check for me again and he told me something like, "Shlooba do wah Kansas teeshka."

Herein lies the problem with understanding the Portuguese language. Contrary to some popular belief, it does not sound like Spanish. I thought I could slip by with my Spanish skills, but I was sadly mistaken. Most of the time, the people there won't even respond to Spanish. They also get pissed when people speak Spanish, like they are trying to make a comparison that shouldn't be made. Portuguese actually sounded a bit like Russian to me.

Tears welled up in my eyes as the attendant spoke because I couldn't understand him. I just couldn't communicate how badly I wanted him to check the lost and found. I actually found myself doing some sort of a pantomime act, putting an imaginary backpack on and trotting around the space in front of the service window. By the grace of God, the attendant brought someone who spoke some English over to help me.

"What callard?" he asked impatiently.

"What?"

He repeated the question with one hand flipped in the air. "Da callard?"

I figured he meant color. "Verde." *Stupid! Abort! No Spanish!* "I mean, green. Green!"

The man sighed and disappeared into a back room. Those minutes waiting felt like decades, as I prayed to God to help me out. Last time I had needed something big, I promised the baby Jesus I wouldn't have sex for the rest of

2009. Standing there, I prayed he'd forgive me for breaking that pledge in Costa Rica.

The waiting pressed on me, not about losing the computer, but about losing Tiny Elvis. *Is it unhealthy to be so attached to a plastic Elvis Presley doll?* I just wanted the guy to come out of the door holding my backpack, though I wasn't holding my breath.

I know the worst-case scenario like I know the way my own skin smells. Loss is ingrained in me like a tattoo only I can see. My anxiety over loss isn't really about the action of the thing going away though. Whether it was my backpack, loved ones, or relationships, loss careens down into a place of wisdom that reminds me of the same thing, over and over again; *I can't control people or outcomes.*

I stood at the window and thought about my baby brother, Dylan, whom I hadn't seen in the nine years... since my father had died. I couldn't believe he was about to turn nineteen. He and I used to be so close. I used to change his diapers and put him on my back to swim him around the lake in our backyard. He was the sweetest thing I'd ever known, and he disappeared from my life shortly after my father died.

I always go back in my head to a meeting with this guy my older brother and I thought was our "family" attorney. Shortly after my dad died, our stepmother told us we needed to go talk to him together because our father didn't have a will. On the day of the meeting, the attorney sat down with my brother, my stepmother, and me, and said, "Your stepmother and I believe you and Ryan should get nothing."

"What do you mean?" I asked.

My former stepmother stared at me with pursed lips.

We knew our dad wouldn't have wanted us to get a ton of money, because he was strong and taught us to be self-sufficient, but he also wouldn't have left us with nothing. *No way.*

"Why?"

"Because he paid for college and he thought that was enough," my former stepmother said.

I had never felt more unimportant and invisible than I did in those moments. I wished my dad could magically appear to stick up for us. He taught us to work hard before we played hard. We had to go to college and get our schoolwork done. He expected us to make something of ourselves, which we did. He had also taught us not to take shit from anyone, which was why there was no way we were about to bow down to being treated that way.

That day, we hired our own attorney through a recommendation from one of my co-workers. Thomas Craven was smart, like my dad. I liked him because he was assertive and passionate about our best interests. He reviewed all of my dad's assets and found that since much of the property and accounts my dad had owned were in his name only, we were legally entitled to a percentage of many of them.

After that, the process moved quickly. Thomas asked the other attorney for a dollar amount and eventually, we received checks that were close to what we'd asked for. My former stepmother's attorney didn't protest because, according to our attorney, we were in the right.

I knew getting to my little brother would be difficult after that. I didn't go into the process without thinking deeply about how my actions could affect my relationship with Dylan. I believed, though, that my former stepmother was looking for a way to push us away and the outcome would have been the same, whether I challenged her or not. When the process ended, I gathered my courage and called her to ask if she'd allow me to take Dylan to the movies. I can still hear her voice, stern and emotionless.

"You will not be seeing him anymore."

"Really? So that's it?"

"You will not be seeing him anymore."

Click.

I thought for weeks about an ambush. I could show up at his school and demand a meeting. Maybe I could sneak him out of the house to go eat burgers and play video games. I couldn't do any of it, though. Dylan was only ten, and I was terrified of scaring and confusing him. With hardly any other family around, his mother would truly become the center of his universe.

Soon after our phone conversation, Dylan's mom took a trip to Montana to visit my father's parents. According to my grandfather, she told him we took her to court, which wasn't true. After that, Grandma and Grandpa stopped talking to us, as well.

My older brother took it harder than me because he had a very close relationship with my grandpa. So, he put a packet together with all of the paperwork and the entire story of what happened from start to finish. He sent it off to my grandpa, but I don't think he read it because he didn't change his mind.

Several months later, we got cards from Grandpa saying he was sorry. He said one of my dad's best friends called him and told him the truth about what happened with my father's money. My grandpa apologized for not believing us. I still don't know which friend called him, but I would thank that friend if I knew who it was.

Dylan used to wake me up at night when I was sixteen and he was two. He slept in my room when I first moved to my dad's and woke up in the middle of the night often. Sometimes, I'd pick him up and read him Shel Silverstein by nightlight.

One time, my dad heard us and came in. "What are you guys doing up?"

"Just reading." We looked up at him, grinning.

He choked up, just watching us. "Okay. Just get him back down soon so you guys aren't tired tomorrow."

I have a little note Dylan wrote me that says, "This is my lucky penny. Have it." There's a penny taped to the note along with a Jolly Rancher. The Jolly Rancher rotted and fell off the paper, but I won't throw it out. I can still see Dylan's face when he gave it to me. It was Easter and he was wearing a goofy shirt with pastel stripes. God, he was cute.

I sent Dylan cards–close to twenty–for his birthday and Christmas every year. I'm not sure if he ever received them. I found him on MySpace a couple years ago and wrote that I would love to hear from him. I was shocked when he wrote back and said he wanted to meet. He said that a couple times, then faded out. I understood his apprehension; his loyalty lay with his mother. I get that. I vowed to just try to be patient. In a way, Dylan was the closest I ever felt to being a mother. Fifteen years his senior, I never experienced having a little person in my life like that. Like missing my father—missing Dylan—still lingers in my stomach like a desperate hunger. It breaks my heart that Dylan is real. He's alive… and I can't touch him.

ɕ

I stood at the ticket window for ten hours (about three minutes). I glared at the door; he didn't come out. I could hear the attendant speaking Portuguese to someone inside. *Please, come out.* He finally did, with my backpack in his arms. I blinked several times, unsure if it was, indeed, my pack.

"No way!" Jumping up and down, I startled the people next to me. If I'd known how to do a backflip in that moment, I would have done several in place. I didn't just hug the attendant; I smothered him. He seemed uncomfortable at first, and then he laughed and patted me on the head.

"Scooby Douche Shliker," I think he said, which roughly translates to, "You dumb American."

"Yes. Yes," I said, patting his arm. "And thank you, too. You are a good man! Great man!"

He watched me skip away, amusement and confusion filling his face.

I know that look well.

When I got into the cab, I put my arms around my pretty pack and exhaled. I must have had a guardian angel or something. How in the world had someone turned it in and not taken anything from inside?

Shannon and I put on pretty dresses that night and enjoyed a delicious non-Portuguese dinner of Caesar salads and club sandwiches to celebrate. Those are our favorite foods… next to pizza. We beamed and laughed over the familiar feast. When we went to bed, I put Tiny E on the pillow next to me. I looked like a ten-year-old, sleeping with my doll, but I didn't care. If this laptop I'm writing on could have fit comfortably in the bed with me, I would have slept with it, too.

Costa Rica Charlie sent me an email the next day and my heart hopped a little. I was feeling joy on the trip, but again, the need to have someone pining over me still crept in, like a late night craving for cinnamon toast.

I am so lucky to have spent that night with you. It was one of the most real encounters I have ever had. I find myself reciting your name, Michelle Elaine Kennedy, I say into sky. What a wonderful night!

Charlie also told me I opened something in his heart. He called me beautiful inside and out and said if I came back to Costa Rica, he would never let me go. He said I inspired him to call his mother, which made my heart soar again. I wrote back and updated him on the trip. I also told him how much I missed him (fantasy). Then, Charlie disappeared again. Each time I checked my email, I hoped. Each time, I ended up disappointed.

I wanted Charlie to read my words and fall in love… and let's face it, validate my worth. I knew deep down he didn't have that power, but I still gave it to him and looked for his emails, anyway. I needed to move on. We had a connection, but he was turning into a ghost, like so many before him.

CHAPTER 9

Angel

SPAIN SMELLS LIKE trees, exhaust, paella, and culture, all mixed together. We started down at the southwestern corner of the country and journeyed on a bus through Madrid. We hadn't planned to go there, but what a good choice it turned out to be.

I adore Picasso and insisted we check out the museum there. Seeing Picasso's original, *Guernica,* for the first time was a mind-bending experience. It's an enormous black and white painting that depicts Picasso's vision of a bombing in the town of Guernica, Spain, in 1937. The piece shows people fighting and reacting with terrified expressions. There is also a colossal horse head, bent back with an open mouth, on one side of the painting. The mural is chaotic and moving. I've seen a lot of art in my life, but *Guernica* is by far the most breathtaking. The composition stretches across an entire wall, and the rest of the rooms around it are devoted to sketches Picasso drew in planning his masterpiece.

Guernica was Myles's favorite painting and one birthday, I bought a print of it for him. I also framed a little painting of two apes. Before I stuck the apes in the frame to give to him, I wrote on the back of the print that I would love him my whole life. I sauntered through the long halls of the museum, wondering why I thought Myles would ever open up the frame and read those words if he didn't know they were there. Better yet, why did I think I would love him my whole life?

I missed Myles, but mostly, I missed being known. There's nothing better than the feeling of someone deeply knowing me. When I agonize over a reoccurring problem, they understand where I'm coming from. They share in my pain. The thing is, a person can't fully empathize if they are self-centered and Myles was. So, did he truly know me? Did I let him? And how self-centered had I been? Had I really let him in?

I thought about whether or not the *Guernica* print hung on his wall in some faraway place. Then, I suddenly wanted to write to Myles or call and tell him I stood inches from the real thing. I wanted Myles to be jealous and remember how much he loved me. I wanted him to break that frame open and read what I wrote. I didn't do anything, though. I let my wants fly out into the air and kept walking.

From Madrid, we headed north to San Sebastian. The hills through Spain aren't very green, but they're stunning, nonetheless. Some are cut like cliffs and others are round and fat with lots of grass and swaying yew trees. I was excited to explore more of the country and confirm the rumors that the Spanish are, indeed, electric and beautiful with svelte physiques and designer clothing. There was an energy and light surrounding Spain. I felt it observing a group of gorgeous men playing basketball on a court off the road. I remembered the exhilaration of moving the ball down the floor as a teenager.

♋

I'm sixteen years old and have just moved to my father's and entered Lodi High School as a junior. I don't know anyone and I'm insecure. I haven't lived here in ten years and I feel out of place. My old high school in the Bay Area is twice the size of this one. I have to show my father I am good at something, so I try out for the basketball team. I played basketball at my other high school and, foolishly, I didn't think I'd have a problem here, but I was wrong.

I hustle and do my best at tryouts, but I fail miserably. My dribbling is sloppy and I miss the shots I take. Beyond that, all the girls in the group are already friends, and it's apparent the team is already decided. When I get home and tell my father I didn't make it, he stews, irate.

"Why can't you and your brother play sports? All I hear is how great you are at basketball and you can't even make a small town team. I'm just really disappointed."

"Why do you say things like that?"

"What did you say?"

I've poked the bear.

"YOU are the one who said you were so great at sports, not me! Looks like I'll never know since you can't even get on a damn team!"

The words pierce like daggers through my heart. My eyes burn. I take a mental snapshot of his frustrated face and make a promise to myself that I will never, ever make my kids feel like garbage for not making it on a stupid basketball team.

୧৮

Exploring the intricately carved streets of San Sebastian, Spain, was like attending the biggest buffet I could imagine, filled with massive amounts of tapas covered with salty meats and gooey cheese. San Sebastian, which is in Northern Spain, near the border of France, is also apparently home to more bars per square mile than any other place in the world. Every establishment we passed displayed colorful plates full of glorious tapas. It was in San Sebastian I decided that keeping my weight down, at least in Spain, would be impossible.

We ate peppers and goat cheese with sun-dried tomatoes. We devoured prosciutto, anchovies, nuts, and mystery meats, all meticulously placed on little pieces of bread. We even accepted when the lady next to us offered up one of her gigantic fried shrimps one day.

Don't mind if I do.

One afternoon, we lay down on a beach full of families running around us and fell asleep in the midst of it all. With bellies full of concoctions we didn't know existed, Shannon and I mellowed into the beauty of the crowd. Many of the kids and moms opted not to wear tops and that didn't seem unusual, either. Sometimes, those moments are the best when you can just unwind into the sand and this life… a parallel universe.

Our first night in San Sebastian, we danced until dawn in a packed night-club. I met Gabrielo in the middle of it all and wrapped my arms around his wide shoulders. He was tall, exotic, and smelled like Drakkar and seventh grade. I wanted to lie next to him and his black head of shoulder length hair and bury my face in his chest, so I did; the larger the man, the more he could erase my anxiety late at night.

Gabrielo held my hand as he walked me up steep hills back to his house. He kept me transfixed with stories of his childhood back in Greece. "I've traveled a lot. I went to Italy at one point and met the American girl. You know, that one who is on the trial in Italy?"

"What trial? Wait… Amanda Knox? The one accused of killing her British roommate? No!"

"Yes. I was looking to share a flat for a semester and I spoke with her and the girl who died. They hated each other. They both told me that. I didn't want to live with them."

"Holy shit! I can't believe you met them. Do you think she's guilty?"

"Who knows?"

The universe seemed so big sometimes, and now it didn't.

"Did they try to subpoena you?

"No. They don't know I know them."

Knox was found guilty, and then she was acquitted. I wondered if his testimony would have mattered.

The moon sparkled on the quiet sea below us as we walked up several streets to get to Gabrielo's flat. He made me a sandwich. It mimicked all the other sandwiches in Spain with a thin piece of ham and an even thinner piece of cheese. Oh, how I missed American sandwiches with eight pounds of glop inside.

Lying with Gabrielo, his massive arms wrapped around my shoulders, I inhaled and imagined the smell was Myles's. He ran his fingers through my hair and I imagined they were attached to Myles's hands. Maybe when I woke up, Gabrielo would be Myles. Sometimes, I thought God sent me random people to briefly remove the ache, because Gabrielo was a dream. I asked him not to try anything and he didn't. He only held me and helped a little as we fell asleep.

ℭ

Every seventeen-year-old's dream is a new car. Mine's a green Toyota Tercel with a stick shift. My new friends at Lodi High School think it's rad. My dad took me to the dealership, knowing I'd never driven stick before, and told me to drive the thing home. He paid the sales guy twenty dollars to take me around nearby streets to show me how to shift gears. I wanted my dad to teach me how to drive the car and wondered why he always assumed I knew everything.

Dealership guy taught me enough to get by. Despite his hour-long tutorial, I ground the gears and almost crashed a dozen times on the forty-mile trek home.

I drove the car for a month and read the manual, but still didn't understand a lot about it. I'm about to go over a bridge by our house on my way to class. I haven't mastered the defroster and when the blazing sun hits the icy windshield, the whole thing fogs up. I'm already up to about fifty miles an hour and I can't see anything in front of me.

I frantically shift the defroster lever back and forth. I can't figure out if the air should be hot or cold. Within ten seconds, the Tercel slams into something and my forehead smacks the steering wheel, hard. Head throbbing, I peek out the side window and discover I've veered into the opposite lane and hit a car coming from the other direction. The whole front sides of both of our vehicles are smashed and smoking.

An ambulance arrives and takes the other driver away. He might be a farm worker. His car is totaled. I'm not sure if mine is or not. Hysterical, I run across the street to our neighbor's house. The couple comforts me and puts an ice pack on my swollen forehead. They call my dad and tell him what happened. I'm afraid of his reaction.

My dad shows up, marches toward me, and punches me in the shoulder. "What is wrong with you? Are you a goddamned idiot? How could you have let this happen? That car is toast. You're done. You're taking the bus now!"

My chin quivers. I am nothing. I think I could have gotten a better reaction if I'd driven the car off a cliff, instead. Maybe...

⚭

Gabrielo and I woke to a rooster crowing outside. My angel got up and grabbed a bag of his favorite pastries, which he had hidden behind his desk so his room-mates wouldn't steal them. I admired the muscles on his naked back as he moved. Gabrielo fed me pieces of bread that were soft and sweet... like him.

My new friend sent me off with kisses and hugs. I knew we would never speak again, but I didn't mind. I only hoped God would send me another pair of arms in a few weeks when the loneliness returned. I prayed that someday, the loneliness would vanish altogether and I could be content in my own skin, all by myself.

⚭

Barcelona is alive and full of statues, buildings, parks, bursting fountains, art, and street performers blanketing the city. We watched Flamenco dancers and Spanish guitar players blow our minds and melt our hearts. The lady who'd rented us our room was totally annoying, but we tried not to let her ruin our mood. Sometimes, Shannon and I would walk in our room to find her inside, making sure the air-conditioning was off. She'd also unplug things when we left them in the socket.

"What in God's name are you doing?" we'd ask.

"Oh, it's okay. It's okay."

"No, it isn't. You can't just be in our room!"

She'd come back in anyway. She wore a mumu and had a little dog that yapped and followed her around everywhere. Sometimes at night, the lady would even knock on our door to tell us to turn the television down.

I got out of that room as much as I could to explore the neighborhoods in Barcelona. The city just moved. I'd watch a street performer dressed like a gargoyle dance for an hour and round the corner to find twenty shops, all selling different versions of Flamenco dresses. I bought one for my sister.

I called her from a payphone near Flamenco Alley and she read me a poem. I cried. My mom told me about everything I'd missed. The dog had gotten sick. Obama won the Peace Prize, and the heat was unbearable. Everything was still happening, just like always.

We pulled another all-nighter at a dance club in Las Ramblas, a popular neighborhood packed with bars, restaurants, and some exceedingly dark corners. We danced until seven in the morning with two guys who appeared out of nowhere. My guy wore a half-buttoned up shirt, that revealed way too much chest hair, and a rosary bead necklace. His hair came to his chin and he continuously slicked it back out of his eyes as he danced. He was dirty hot, like he belonged in a salsa dancing studio... or possibly my bed.

Strangely, I never even talked to my dude. We simply danced through the night in silence. He spun me around, grabbing my waist—thighs, face, back, neck, possibly my boob—and entertained me until the sun came up and the place closed. With puppy dog eyes, he asked to come over at the end of the night. "My roommate. She the only one with key. I have nowhere to go."

In the light of day, I wondered if I needed anything else. Latin Guy's octopus arms coupled with the exhilaration of dancing felt incredible, but I didn't want any more closeness. Sweaty and disheveled, I stared at the fresh sunlight bouncing through the trees and onto Antonio Banderas's face. I could take that statuesque body home and use it as a bandage for my broken heart, but I knew when the bandage got ripped off and Dude left, my wound would still be there, pulsating and begging me to JUST DEAL WITH IT, MICHELLE! So, I decided to suck it up for once and survive on my own without the warm-body-security-blanket next to me. As Shannon and I walked home, I felt numb.

CHAPTER 10

I'll Show You

OUR PLAN IN Croatia was to land in a magnificent coastal town called Dubrovnik where a man from the hostel we booked would pick us up. Shannon and I posted up outside the airport terminal to wait.

"The guy is supposed to be holding a sign with my name on it," I told Shannon.

"Sweet. I've always wanted someone to hold up a sign for me."

"Me, too. It's weird. The hostel guy who emailed me said he would be carrying a table with my name on it. I'm assuming it won't be a table, though."

We laughed and continued searching for him.

"On the hotel application, they asked for my ethnicity. I said Samoan. He probably won't be looking for a blond dipstick like me."

"Why do you always say you're something else?"

"I guess I just don't understand why they're even asking about my ethnicity, so I say I'm from Iceland, Chile, or anywhere else I'd like to go. This might be the only time I should have told the truth."

A buxom Croatian lady walked by us into the terminal. The woman stepped up near Shannon and lost her footing, almost falling on her butt.

"That lady almost ate shit. Man, that was funny," Shannon whispered.

"Crap. I didn't see." I looked back and saw her wearing high-waisted mom jeans, a white blouse, and white Keds. She searched around the terminal, confused.

"I wonder if she is looking for us." As the words came out of my mouth, the woman turned around, approached us, and un-crumpled a piece of notebook paper with my name written on it. I had my camera in hand to take a picture of the sign, but at that moment, it seemed weird and silly, so I quietly put it back in my bag.

"Are you Michelle?"

"Oh, hi. Yes," I replied, relieved.

"My neighbor over there. He take us to room."

We made our way to the car and realized how different this country was from Spain and how little money this woman and her neighbor had. Their Datsun was almost too small to hold our luggage, and I was afraid our driver wouldn't be able to fit it in the trunk. He got out of the car with a cigarette hanging from his lip. With disheveled hair and a button-up shirt covered in food stains, he managed to shove almost everything in. We put the rest on our laps in the back seat.

Fuzz, dust, and cigarette ashes canvassed the upholstery inside the car. Once it took off, the passenger seat in front of me rolled back into my legs. I asked the woman to try and set it, but after several failed attempts, I told her to just forget it.

The woman pointed to the tops of miniature castles built along a cliff below the road. "This the old town. We have rain, but it gone. My neighbor nice to take us."

"Oh, yes. Definitely. Thank you, Sir," I said.

He grunted, kept driving, and steered the Datsun around several corners, as the woman continued her tour.

"This shopping area and pizza you can go." She pointed to different places. Naturally, I tried to take mental notes of the pizza place's location. "This road go back way to old town." She pointed again.

85

Dubrovnik is situated on the coast above gorgeous cliffs, cute little shops, and restaurants on the water. What makes it unique is this ancient castle structure that sits right in the middle of it all. You walk across a bridge and through an overhang straight out of a *Game of Thrones* episode—they really do shoot scenes there—to get inside. Then, you twist and turn, around more restaurants and all sorts of eclectic little art displays and shops.

The castle city was built in the seventh century—a gazillion years ago. Its stony streets, churches, and secret passageways withstood earthquakes and wars. Getting lost there ruled. We just had to be careful in flip-flops because the slippery granite was treacherous. And yes, I fell on my face.

The car wound down a narrow street lined with apartments stacked high on another cliff. Hundreds of concrete steps led up to the majority of the buildings; getting up those steps with our bags would be treacherous.

"Okay. We here," the lady announced.

"Kill me now," I whispered to Shannon.

We reluctantly grabbed our suitcases and hiked up to the hostel. The outside steps led to inside steps and we quickly found out our building had no elevator.

Shannon counted and as it turned out, we climbed more than 106 steps. Yes, she counted. She just does stuff like that sometimes.

Huffing and puffing, we made it to the apartment entrance. Plants lined the door and we could hear an elderly woman inside yelling something in Croatian. Then, our host opened the door and we discovered our fate. She waved her arm and opened another door to a bedroom right by the front entrance. "Welcome. Here your room!"

I found it hard to concentrate through the pot roast cloud wafting from the kitchen. Dishes clanked as the kitchen lady's voice boomed down the hall. Then it hit us; this was a family home and grandma was cooking Sunday dinner.

"Here dee bathroom you use. Laundry fifty Kuna. I do laundry you and hang it and fold."

Wide-eyed and confused, we scanned the apartment. We had not signed up to stay in someone's house, let alone share a family bathroom. Embarrassed, we thanked the woman, slipped into our wing, and shut the door.

"Holy shit! This is like a family's house! What is happening?" I asked Shannon.

"Dude, didn't the reservation form say it was for a hostel with a private bathroom? This is their house. This is creepy, right?"

The grandma yelled more things in Croatian from the kitchen. A plate broke and Grandma's volume intensified.

"Taj bog pot roast, ash KUHA Timberlake!" is pretty close to what she said.

"Of course! I would never knowingly book a room in someone's house, but we paid online through that hostel booker site. What should we do?" A door slammed and another family member went into the bathroom across the hall.

"I don't know. That lady is nice. I feel bad and I really need my clothes washed. Deeply," Shannon said.

We agreed that carrying our shit back down the stairs would be too much to bear and we could stick it out for one night. It seemed like a solid plan until Shannon changed her shirt and our host barged in without knocking.

The lady proudly handed us a plate of donuts. "My mother, she make these for you. Plum cakes!"

I held the plate as the woman launched into another tutorial of the city on a paper map in her hand. She pointed to different city sights as Shannon stood frozen, holding her shirt over her naked chest. Adding to the awkwardness, the woman's nipple slipped out of her bra and protruded underneath a thin white blouse. We tried not to stare, but found it impossible. The nipple bore the resemblance of a peach Dots candy under a transparent veil of silk. Finally, she finished talking, walked out, and closed the door.

"What the hell, Michelle? I just saw her boob! Did you see that?"

"Of course, I did. How could I not? And what's the deal? She just walks right in here?"

"Dude, that thing looked like a little baby's finger."

"That thing looked like a pink mini-gherkin."

"That thing looked like a crunched up pile of rubber cement."

"No, that thing... Dude, try this." I handed Shannon the plate of mystery donuts. I had inhaled one and couldn't think anymore.

"Holy shit!" A powdered sugar mustache formed on her upper lip.

"I know, right?" Those donuts, all sticky and fresh, changed everything.

"Don't be afraid to get them in that sugar there. It's incredible."

The thought of staying for the sole purpose of eating the grandma's food crossed my mind, then left. We needed to get out of there.

When I finished stuffing my face, I tiptoed across the hall to check out the bathroom. Inside, quirky knick-knacks lined shelves above a pink washer and dryer. A crooked clown painting hung over towels that stuck to the floor in the corner. The bathtub was cracked in places and didn't have a showerhead. I was pretty sure I saw a finger in the garbage can, too. Not really, but I could have. The strangest thing about the bathroom was that it belonged to a family, and their crusty toothpaste stains and dirty clothes marked it in a way that made me not want to be in there.

After I gave Shannon the depressing bathroom report, we surrendered, gave our clothes to our host, and paid her to wash them. Exhausted, we collapsed on the bed and fell asleep. We dozed for hours.

When we woke, we had some unusual, but understandable, dreams to report.

"Okay, I dreamt I went to the bathroom and couldn't find my way back to our room, and I walked in on some naked man sleeping in another room. Then, I couldn't escape and I had to crawl under the door," Shannon said.

"Well, I dreamt that the boob lady came in and told us the only television in the house was the one in our room and her son needed to watch his favorite show in here with us at eight o' clock."

"Let's go get some pizza."

"Oh, yeah! I totally remember the directions."

It was the best idea of the day. As we made our way down the stairs and into the street, I looked up and saw our clothes, hanging from a line far up on a hilltop. I assumed it was in the backyard of the house. Maybe a small airplane could get us up there. My yellow dress looked like a little banana, blowing in the wind. Thank God, I had clean clothes, for once. Maybe the grandma could make us some more donuts for the road.

It's strange to me now that we segued from the random family's apartment to staying at some of the most luxurious hotels Croatia had to offer. Shannon's best friend, Brett, came to visit us from Atlanta, as promised, and she used her airline points to hook us up at some five-star establishments. She flew extensively for work, so she had millions of points to spend on rooms.

In another coastal town, Split, we swam in infinity pools and sipped Mojitos by the sea. I even won twenty dollars playing roulette at a hotel casino. The three of us ate caviar and calamari and slept in beds draped in fresh linens and fluffy pillows. It would definitely hurt to go back to the grubby—yet affordable—hostels, but I tried to stay in the moment. We had to make our money last through the entire trip, so hostels would have to do.

We dove into our favorite day in Croatia around the island, Hvar. The Adriatic Sea was cobalt blue, like a lake. The sand was rocky and the vibe reminded me of Greece. We found a dock and decided to see how boisterous we could look jumping off. As each of us jumped, the other two captured pictures of the leap into the water.

"Turn more toward me," Brett advised.

"Shannon, swivel your head and curve your back more," I yelled, holding the camera to my face. She vaulted over the water and I clicked the button again and again.

We took close to one hundred photographs; amusing ourselves for hours. To follow it up, we raced each other in the water on the five-dollar floaties we purchased at a convenience store.

With determination to win, Shannon announced the rules. "Okay. Just arms!" she yelled. "Legs have to stay on the floatie. We go from here to that dock."

We raced back and forth through every type of competition we could concoct. No arms. No legs. Both arms and legs, but you had to stay on the floatie. I never won, but I came close, and it bothered me. I'm so competitive. I felt weak. Then, I tried to remember that the gratification of traveling and enjoying myself were all that mattered.

That night, we pulled out dresses and got pretty. After I blew my hair out, I felt clean and less rug-rattish. It was nice to wear lipstick and feel a dress twirling around my knees. Hanging with someone who could tell us new stories mixed things up, as well.

Brett, with her chocolate skin, almond eyes, and beautiful smile, was a pleasure to be around, not to mention the fact that she booked the rooms and set the schedule that week so we just had to relax and enjoy ourselves. It was calming for Shannon, too, having her best friend there. Brett made me miss my best friend, but Jessica had a new baby to care for and she hadn't been able to come, so that was that.

I fell asleep that night with a belly full of fish and had horrible dreams. I couldn't understand why because my five-star bed ruled. I guess my subconscious didn't care about those things. It went where it wanted, when it wanted.

❧

I am running with Dylan through the grass behind my father's house. My dad is on the tractor and the dog is jumping around us. I am playing with ghosts again and I know it. One ghost is real; the other isn't a ghost at all.

Suddenly, I'm eighteen years old and my father and I are fighting in my bedroom. Dylan is trying to stop my father and me from screaming at each other.

❧

I jolted up and quickly scanned the dark room, wondering where I was. I made out the forms of Shannon and Brett sleeping soundly and took a deep breath. I slumped back onto the bed but couldn't unstick myself from the memory of the worst night between my father and me.

It started out with my drunken dad knocking on my bedroom door. I was getting ready for bed and things had been strained between us. A few months into my first serious relationship, my dad admitted he wanted to spend more time with me. I, on the other hand, just wanted to be with my boyfriend.

My dad, in his infinite struggle to get me to lose weight, bet me $200 I couldn't lose twenty pounds. I wasn't fat; my father simply wanted me to be really thin. If I won, I got $200. If he won, I had to give him twenty foot rubs. I

90

didn't lose the weight and he won the bet. His knocking irritated me because I wanted to go to sleep. I mouthed off and he yelled back.

The screaming intensified when he didn't get his way. "You lost the bet! You need to pay up!"

"Not now! I don't want to touch your feet right now, God!"

Our conversation then dipped into the Rolodex of the worst of parent phrases. "If you don't like it here, you can leave!"

I despised that saying more than any other. It always made me feel like he actually wanted me to leave. Furious, I screamed back, coming down to his level. "Oh, yeah? I hate you! How 'bout that?" Destroyed, I wondered how we had gotten there.

Didn't he care if I left?

I choked on sobs as my barely-out-of-diapers brother stood between us, pleading. "Leave my sister alone!"

My stepmother stood next to him, begging my father and me to stop.

Ignoring their pleas, my father turned his fist sideways, like he was pounding on a locked door, and hammered it into my nose.

My stepmother picked my brother up and rushed him to another room.

Blood dripped out of my nose and I thought the world had stopped. The man I worshiped made me bleed on the inside more than the outside. Horrified, I wiped the blood with the back of my hand. How would we recover from this?

My dad stared at me, stunned, as tears mixed with the crimson on my face. I felt my heart breaking. "I hate you! You want me out? I'm gone!"

I'll show you.

Before my father could even respond, I grabbed some of my things, shoved them in a suitcase at warp speed, and ran to my car, my nightgown whipping my legs. I headed to my boyfriend's parent's house. I wanted my dad to chase after me, but he didn't.

I went back the next day to pack the rest of my things. I'm not sure what my plan was, beyond staying with my boyfriend's family. *Insert Lifetime movie clip.*

My dad got up from his office chair when I walked in. His face looked hopeful. I could tell he wanted to make up, but I was determined to make him pay. I packed the rest of my clothes, said goodbye, and bolted out.

As my boyfriend and I drove away, the ache pounded so strongly in my bones, I thought I might disintegrate. A part of me hoped he would run after me this time. He didn't. Through my tears, I saw my father, holding the curtain and looking out his office window at me. I knew he hurt, too. At the time, I just wondered why he didn't love me enough to not hurt me.

I wish I could go back to that night and just rub his feet. I want to make it better for him as much as I want to make it better for myself. I nodded off again, hoping to picture something that hurt less.

⅌

I'm standing in our field, searching in the dark for a screaming lamb. The air is so black, I can barely make out blood dots on the grass by my feet. I follow the dots but can't find the lamb. I want to help the lamb and stop the bleeding. I run around, trying to locate the sounds. Every time I think I'm close, the scream moves farther away.

CHAPTER 11

Ghosts

In Italy, my invisible travel partner would not leave my side. Strangely, the hotel we booked reminded me so much of my father, the memories pressed against my chest. My dad had never traveled to Italy, yet I felt him in the air and could smell him walking by me. Had I opened the floodgates too wide? I wasn't sure, but it was nothing short of magical being there.

We ended up at a farm in the middle of nowhere and everywhere in Tuscany. We drove for miles to get to the entrance, then turned down a narrow dirt road that took us even farther into the sticks. Approaching the property, we saw buildings shaped like intricate castles, all covered with ivy, flowers, and windows with wooden shutters. Vineyards lined the grounds along rolling hills of olive trees. The place was like something out of an Italian fairytale, complete with speckled pigs and feral cats creeping around shaggy dogs, napping in the sun.

We found our room up a marble staircase and past an old library with shelves upon shelves of dusty books. I loved the library and wanted nothing more than to write in there. The stairs creaked and the shutters banged against the building when the breeze kicked up. At night, thunder rolled and lightning peeked into our room as if to say, "This place could be haunted."

Dinners were a family affair; fifteen hotel guests sat along wooden tables, guzzling Chianti made from grapes growing outside. Our first night, we enjoyed fresh pesto, and I don't mind if I had three helpings. My belly, at that point, was popping out of my pants like a life ring. I couldn't help it as trays of gnocchi and veal begged me to take just one more bite. The entire place reeked of garlic, basil, and pure heaven. Italian women cooked all day, and not a moment passed when my nostrils couldn't make love to the aromas.

One night, we finished with fresh lemon cake and sleepwalked upstairs to bed. I dozed off to visions of burrata and heirlooms, only to wake up to a room so opaque, I couldn't see my hand in front of my face. Terrified of ghosts, I put Tiny Elvis on the nightstand next to me and opened the shutters enough to let some moonlight in. The floor creaked and I tried to detect any movement in the room.

At one point, I felt three taps on my shoulder and begged my dad to protect me. Holding my breath, I jerked at every eerie sound. My heart pounded so fast, I had to turn the bathroom light on to sleep, which resulted in me staring at the bathroom door, sure Frankenstein would walk through it. I was angry at myself for being scared because I loved it there so much. Somehow, I fell back to sleep, but couldn't begin to think about the next night and the next; we were scheduled to stay for a week.

"It's no joke," I told Shannon the next morning. "This fricken' tap on my shoulder happens and I'm wide awake, wondering what the hell to do."

"That's weird because I felt something on my neck."

"What? This has never happened to me. I'm pissed, too, because I love this place. I don't want to be scared."

"I didn't feel scared, though. Like it was a nice ghost or something," Shannon said.

"Nice or not, I'm freaked out."

The hotel owners told us about the ghost of a woman named Maya who apparently haunted the wing outside our room. Maya had lived in the building years before when she was forced to marry a man she didn't love. Lost in a sea of depression, she apparently jumped off a nearby bridge to her death. Maybe Maya tapped me on the shoulder to tell me she knows sadness, too.

The following day started with a tour of the garden. Sloshing through wet dirt, I watched raindrops roll off green leaves and onto the ground, but the light rain didn't bother me. The garden exploded with color and I wanted to drink it in. Blue jays chirped and the air blew clean as sunlight peeked through mushy clouds. Mud dots painted my calves and everything smelled fresh.

Freda, the old Italian woman who oversaw the garden, showed us around. She knew everything about organic vegetables and things like perennials and mulch. Half the time, I had no idea what she was talking about, but I didn't care because the onions smelled spicy and the tomatoes shined like red hearts on the vine.

Freda pointed to a hole where something had pooped and dug. "Dis lettuce is ruined by wild animal." She showed us a fence she'd built, and where she tried to cover it with wire so deer wouldn't crawl through, but it hadn't worked; the deer just started hopping over it.

Our guide had the dirty fingernails of a woman who cared. Mud caked around her rain boots and leaves lodged in her hair. Years of gardening showed on her face, but she looked exquisite to me. I could have listened to her talk all day.

When Freda grabbed a tree and told us to identify it, I closed my eyes and sailed back to age nine.

♍

I'm riding in my dad's truck with the wind blowing my hair back from my face. We're listening to country music and my father is singing it all twangy to make me laugh.

"Allllll my ex's live in Texas."

Hay is stacked high in the pastures beside us and it smells like home.

Dad asks me to name trees and plants. "You gotta learn these, sweetie. Your dad's a farmer. You need to know your trees!"

෯

I looked at Freda then back to the branches and the shiny orange balls hanging from them. "Persimmon!"

"That's my girl."

"Thanks, Dad."

After I chased a few cats and ate dusty cherry tomatoes off the vine, we retreated to the kitchen. When we arrived at 10:00 am, the chefs told us the process of cooking our feast would take upwards of three hours.

I laughed and thought of my mother, telling me to have patience. She'd pushed to teach me how to make Thanksgiving dinner for as long as I could remember. "It takes me a week for a reason, Michelle," she'd say. "You will do this yourself one day and I won't be here to help you."

I always told my Mom I would learn how to make the dinner when I grew up. At thirty-three, I guessed that day hadn't come yet because the three-hour session was about to be the most time I'd ever spent in a kitchen. Working in television news for so long, I got accustomed to reporting at night and getting food to go; I'd never made the time to cook.

Our menu included gnocchi with roasted bell pepper sauce, complemented by a saltimbocca with veal and cheese rolled up inside. We also made a dessert called Chocolate Salami. Confused, I asked the cooks why in the world they would put chocolate with salami. They laughed and told me to read the ingredients. Apparently, when you crunch crackers up with chocolate then roll the dough and cut it into thin circles, it resembles salami. The dessert wouldn't actually have salty meat inside.

The one older cook didn't speak a stitch of English, so she used a translator. I couldn't be sure, but I think the main lady liked my chopping skills and might have thought me to be the best in the class (there were three of us). I minced my zucchini the finest and peeled potatoes with sheer elegance. When it came time to roll the dumplings, I think I knocked it right out of the park.

Head Cook Lady whispered to her helper, and she may have said something along the lines of, "This girl is really surprising me," or, "This one is nothing short of amazing." When we sat down to devour our three courses, I think it might have gone a little like, "This girl can eat!" I kept surprising them.

The food we made tasted so good, I wanted to cry.

Maybe I did.

Truth be told, I can eat heaps. I'd let the battle between my love for food and love for a fit body drag out for too many years. The fact that Shannon and I spent most days lounging around like sloths didn't aid in muffin-top eradication. I'd gained at least ten pounds since we'd left. Sadly, I used to think I was fat five years and twenty pounds ago. Now, I was adjusting to a belly I didn't use to have and some new chub on my back. How in the hell did "back fat" happen? *Well, Michelle, it's called pizza, ranch, those peanut butter pretzels from Trader Joes, and beer.*

Two strapping lads from New York arrived our third night there. I was writing in the library (and daydreaming about dinner) when they appeared on a tour of the property. From the moment I spotted the freshies, I had a feeling we'd spend time with them that night. They smiled and made eye contact. I said hello.

A red-haired behemoth and a skinny blond, both were tall and built for rolling around on linen sheets. Hugh, the blond, was a little on the thin side. I mean, he wasn't anorexic, but my insecure-self preferred larger men. Tom had cute dimples and smelled good.

After they left, I ran to our room and told Shannon to get dressed. I was excited to hang out with those guys because the rest of the guests at the hotel weren't our speed. They were nice, but mostly young hipsters from Maine studying sustainability in Italy. *Need I say more?*

We cleaned up–brushed our hair and put on some lip gloss–and showed up to pre-dinner winetasting with bells on. To my delight, as our guys poured Sangiovese next to us, some of the "sustainabilitators" struck up a conversation.

"So, are you the brave girls who quit your jobs to travel all around the world?" a gal named Chrissy asked.

"Why, yes. Yes, we are," I replied.

And keep it coming, my eco-friendly friend. Let these guys hear juuuust how awesome we are before we even meet them.

We were, in fact, so bombarded at dinner, our new imaginary boyfriends couldn't get a word in edgewise. By the time dinner ended, we stewed a bit over our guys not trying harder to make their way to our section.

"I'm not talking to them first," I told Shannon.

"Oh, hells no."

"Whatever. They're dumb." *And I'm a child.*

I took my nineteenth sip of wine. Free wine flowed until the bottles from dinner ran out. During dinner, the guys had purchased five extra bottles, which they lined up in front of them like lures of bait. Some of the hipsters converged around both the bottles and the guys. Jealousy bit me as I wondered if I'd be drinking that wine.

Most of the group retreated to an after-dinner discussion on composting and Shannon went to the bathroom, leaving me alone at our table. Unable to avoid it, the guys and I finally made eye contact and they waved me over. Mission accomplished. *And oh, yes. All that wine is mine. Well, at least two bottles.*

Wine drinking segued into conversation and a bit of a duel out on the patio. Hipster Girl, with tie-dyed bandana, showed up after the composting meeting and worked her flirting skills at the table. About ten of us had moved outside to smoke, drink, and tell stories under a grapevine-lined wooden patio cover. Hipster Girl, who was all of nineteen, kept trying to talk to both guys, but we weren't going down without a fight.

Shannon told jokes to Tom with the dimples, as I got to know Hugh, the one who maybe needed to eat some more gnocchi Bolognese. We shot the usual shit.

"So, what do you do?"

"Where have you traveled?"

"How old are you?"

Yep. That one came up and not by me. He was twenty-six.

I think we were in one of those *Annie Hall* moments, where you listen to the dialogue in your head above anything else. *Would I sleep with him? Are my teeth purple from the wine? Do I have gas? Does he think I'm old? Do I look as old as I am?*

Hugh eventually grabbed my hand and gently pulled me inside. He pressed me against the wall of the candlelit entryway and suddenly didn't seem so skinny. Kissing him, I wondered if the wine had warped my perceptions. Did I want him, specifically, or was that old need to connect as present as the ghosts swimming through the air around us?

Quit thinking, Michelle.

Hugh spoke with a bit of a lisp through gleaming white teeth and a show-stopping smile. Although thin, he towered above me, so I temporarily got over my size issues. Did he remind me of my youth? Did he buy that I was twenty-eight? If I told him he looked like Anthony Michael Hall in *Weird Science*, would he even know what I meant?

I grabbed his Johnson and stopped caring. What a big surprise. Back in our room, I remembered honesty is the best policy. In my best Elvis voice, I told him, "Hugh, that thing is huuuuge."

He laughed and grabbed a condom. Then, about thirty intoxicated seconds into it, he asked if we could take the condom off.

"No can do, Hugh. We don't know each other."

"You're totally right. Sorry."

"Can we just snuggle and call it a night?"

"Of course."

Hugh put his arms around me and I exhaled.

I thought again about his age. When I'd graduated high school, he had been an eleven-year-old, building clay volcanoes in the sixth grade. *God, help me.* I just hoped he thought I was smart and pretty. *Jesus, Michelle. Shut your yapper.*

After our sort-of sex, the unexplainable demon noises rolled back in. The floor squeaked and we heard faint knocks on the dresser. Hugh and I held each other in silence, our hearts beating into one another's chests.

Next, I did something really dumb and totally ripped off from a fake reality ghost hunting show I saw once. "If there are any ghosts in this room, make your presence known and get it over with," I said to the air.

"Are you crazy?"

"A little?" *If only he knew.*

My advice? Don't do this when you're intoxicated at a ghost hotel because as soon as the words came out, the doorknob to our room jiggled against the lock. We stopped breathing. The whites of our eyes gleamed in the dark, like Pee-wee Herman lost in the desert.

"I can't stay in here," Hugh whispered.

"Don't leave me. You can't leave!" My voice shook. I honestly didn't need Hugh to fill any void that evening; I just didn't want to get killed by Damien by myself.

By some miracle, Hugh and I finally passed out. When we woke, his arms felt weird around my naked body. He was adorable. He was just so young and thin; my insecurities slept right there on the pillow with us. When Hugh got out of bed, I threw his boxers at him and said I had fun.

He told me he would see me at breakfast.

I never went.

My weight and age continued to consume my thoughts. During our travels, we were surrounded by twenty-somethings on a daily basis. Not many thirty-two and thirty-three-year-olds quit their lives to travel the world, so the "ten-years-younger-thans" were everywhere, flaunting their energy, stamina, and sculpted abdominal muscles every day and night. I didn't hate the youngsters, but I knew my days as a twenty-year-old, dancing on tables, were long gone. Granted, if I felt like dancing on a table, I would, but I just didn't. Did that mean I'd transitioned from Miss to Ma'am for real?

Shit.

My need to swing from the rafters had morphed into a desire to listen to Amos Lee (swoon), drink wine, and share stories. The transition was liberating, but it also made me blue. That time wouldn't come back. I wouldn't go to Cabo San Lucas with my girlfriends and watch men drink shots off my chest. *No big loss there.* I wouldn't be able to eat five hamburgers and not gain five pounds. *Huge loss.* I wouldn't hear someone say, "Oh, you're still so young." Most of all, I wouldn't have my twenties fanned out in front of me like dominos of endless possibilities. *Deep sigh.* Some of it felt really depressing. On the bright side, I would never have been able to handle a trip like ours, financially or emotionally, at twenty-five, either. There is the yin and yang to it, I guess.

Once Hugh left, I pulled the covers over my head and fell into a deep sleep. I slept better when the ghosts vaporized in the daylight. Unfortunately, my dreams forced me to deal with another ghost. His name was Michael Kennedy, and I missed him so.

❀

In my dream, I'm back at my father's house, waiting for him to come through the garage door. I hear his truck door close and he blows into the house, smelling like bourbon. In a flash, he's in the kitchen, pulling food out of the freezer to make a dinner containing meat and meat.

"Put Star Trek on," he tells me.

He's wearing his red plaid flannel tucked into Levis. Unwrapping frozen grub, he kicks off his boots and walks around in thick white socks. His cigar hangs from his lip. As always, he towers above me.

My friend, Lindsay, is over. My dad is frying antelope burgers and preparing oven fries. We want to watch Friends and he wants to watch Star Trek, so with plate in hand, he goes upstairs to watch the television in his room. I kiss him goodnight. I want to give him the remote so he'll stay downstairs with us. I want to hear his laughter fill the room. I want the thing that's coming to pass us by.

This all happened the last night I saw my dad alive. In my dream, I'm suddenly waiting again at the garage door, knowing he will never walk back through it. I will never see his face and I will never bounce onto his lap to bug him and make him laugh. He's dead. His driver's license picture and the accident are breaking news on the television screen, and my little brother is crying. I'm waiting for someone to tell us it isn't real.

"Please, tell me it isn't real," Dylan sobs.

"You read my mind."

❀

Sometimes I wonder which person I am waiting for. My dad? Costa Rica Charlie? Myles? Any man with a pulse? I do know I've learned, over and over again, that the one-night stand doesn't add anything to my life. If I could simply enjoy the sex and not freak out about everything—my body, my words, my age—it would be different… better. It's like drinking too much wine or eating an entire pizza—I feel fantastic briefly, until I crash down into shame oblivion. The self-hatred spiral that follows makes me feel worse than before. I can't win, but like with the pizza, I continually go back for more, even though I know it will hurt me in the long run.

It's like that game siblings play where the older, bigger one takes the younger one's hand and turns it back on himself. "Why are you hitting yourself? Why do you keep hitting yourself?" I ask myself that question, but I can't find the answer.

I don't believe it's a coincidence I pulled Erica Jong's *Fear of Flying* out of a shared book basket in my favorite library. In her 1973 novel, Jong explores the quest for a "zipless fuck," an amazing and random sexual experience with a stranger. It's the sex we fantasize about, all hot and disease-free on a counter top or train. It's the greatest sex, with no strings attached. Unfortunately, Jong's protagonist recognizes this kind of sex doesn't really exist. Inevitably, a dick goes limp or the train ride gets too bumpy. One-night stands rarely go the way we want.

Jong examines the contradictory needs for security with a man and single-hood in a chapter called, "Seduced and Abandoned." Like me, Jong's main character has conversations with herself.

"Me: Why is being alone so terrible?
Me: Because if no man loves me, I have no identity.
Me: But obviously that isn't true."

Jong wrote these words before I was born, but the struggle continues for many of us. I want the security blanket, and I want to be fine, all by myself, at the same time. I want hot sex with a stranger, but I don't want to need anything from him afterwards. I want Myles back, even though I don't. He's a need without a face. He's an imaginary body I hold onto to feel secure. In reality, he hadn't actually made me feel taken care of. I hung on to the idea of him to keep connected to that body and pulse, but I hadn't seen that body or face for a long time. *I'm holding on to an illusion.*

I'm a child who can't let go of her blanket. The parents keep cutting the blanket down so over time, the child will only have a diminutive square to hold. I'm grabbing on so tightly to my square, my hands are bleeding. When I look, I realize the square isn't even there anymore. It flew away when Myles left.

Let him go, Michelle. He's not security; he is pain. He makes your hands bleed. Actually, you make your own hands bleed.

As Shannon drove our rental car around orange Tuscan hills lined with sunflowers and olive trees, it occurred to me that the ghosts I encountered might be my own. I was examining and bringing the scariest parts of myself to the surface. I was also sifting through my relationship with my father more than his actual death. I thought I was supposed to face his death and grieve, when in reality, I needed to understand our relationship and how it shaped me.

I think I released my own demons in Italy and they were pestering me in the night. It's strange to wrap my head around, but it could be true. I hadn't been brave enough to face anything before the trip. Maybe, if I kept trying my hardest, the ghosts would go away. Or maybe, if I got to know them better, they wouldn't scare me anymore.

♑

I scheduled a massage the day before we left Italy. A flier on the front desk of our villa convinced me to try Shiatsu for the first time. The brochure said a guy would come to the hotel and set his table up in the library. That seemed fine since I'd already spent so much time writing in there already.

When he arrived, the masseur and I headed to the library, where I stood by the window as he set up. I breathed the hills of Northern Italy in for the last time. What a magnificent place. I wondered in that moment if I'd ever taste olive oil like that again. I certainly felt better than I had when we'd first arrived.

"Thank you, God," I whispered.

A cat crept along the peach-colored building below me. An eagle screeched from high in the clouds. The Bolognese cooking downstairs wafted through the window into my mouth. With a silly grin plastered on my face, I turned around to check on massage guy's progress and saw it—a bat the size of a black puppy flew around the room in a silent frenzy. Each time it circled, the flying rat-beast came within inches of my head. It had apparently entered through the fireplace.

"Oh, God! Jesus! God and Jesusssss!" I screamed, dropping like liquid into the wood floor.

"'Tis okay. It just a bat."

Just a bat? Is he mental?

"I can't! I'm too scared!" If I'd contracted rabies from a bat in a library, I would have been so pissed. Here I was, all giddy and serene, and this bat blew in there, ruining my sweet and special moment. Man, I'm afraid of bats.

I wanted to go for the door, but I figured the bat would run into my mouth at least a few times on its way around the room. Maybe its sonar feature would tell it not to grab onto my face and chomp, but there was no way of knowing. I didn't want to have to get a rabies shot in the stomach. Lying there like a limp pancake, I wondered what to do.

While I tried to figure it out, massage guy attempted to shoo the bat out the window right above me. That was all I needed. Terrified, I shut my eyes and crawled to the door. I don't know how close I came to the bat because I couldn't see. I escaped, opened my eyes, and scooted down the hall to our room to find Shannon, reading on her bed.

"It's a bat!" I shrieked.

"What? Where?"

"In the library!" A couple of deep breaths later, I ran back down the hall to see if massage guy had gotten the job done. He swung the door open as I approached.

"Bat gone!" he cheered. I meticulously scanned the room to make sure the bat wasn't hiding in a lampshade. The window was wide open and I couldn't see any bat.

My hero. The massage was good, too.

Intermission

WE ARE AT the halfway point here and I want to take this time to answer some of your questions. No, I don't read minds, but I think I can guess what you are wondering.

- How often did you wash your underwear, Michelle?
- Did you have enough money? And dang it why won't you tell us how much you spent in total?
- Were you talking to Shannon about all this inner turmoil? Did she think you were a real drag? Did she deal with struggles, too?
- Did the whole "booking hostels as you went" thing actually work?

We washed our underwear in the sinks of hostels and hung them to dry near the windows and washed the rest of our clothes every week and a half at public Laundromats. Yes, our rooms with clotheslines hanging outside of them often resembled a shantytown, but we didn't care. We packed too much stuff, so we whittled our supply down in the end to one pair of jeans and a sweater each, as well as a couple of shirts and undergarments. You quickly learn how much you *don't* need on a trip like that.

I've debated revealing how much money I spent because I've heard stories about travelers surviving for an entire year on $5,000. I spent a lot more than $5,000 over the nearly six months we were gone. We were smart and frugal, with the exception of some adventure sport activities and a weeklong boat trip through the Great Barrier Reef (details to come), but again, $5,000 would never have cut it. Keep in mind, we traveled through eleven countries, took around twenty plane flights, several trains, and even a ship from Croatia to Italy. All in all, I spent $30,000. Some money I'd saved, and the rest I received from my dad's accident settlement.

For the most part, we stayed in hostels, shared bathrooms, and didn't dine lavishly. We splurged occasionally, but overall, we managed our money quite well. Some travelers couch surf, sleep in dorms with twenty other people, don't eat much, hitch rides, and stay in the same country. I think that saves money, but that wasn't our trip. We traveled the world over for 152 days.

I did speak with Shannon about my internal struggles. She was supportive and relayed many of her own feelings. My friend and I are incredibly close and share almost everything. That said, I'd been living with the pain of my father's death for many years and while I am spilling my guts about it all on these pages, I still had the time of my life on the trip. It's possible to feel deep anguish on the inside and still amuse myself on the outside. The bulk of my struggles, I wrote down and processed myself.

Shannon sifted through stuff of her own on the trip; it was impossible not to. However, the reason I don't write more about Shannon's personal life is because she asked me not to. Unlike me, she's a private person and doesn't spill her guts easily. I respect and love her very much, so I honored her request and kept the more personal anecdotes limited to good old Michelle Kennedy.

When Shannon and I planned the trip, we talked extensively about writing a book together. We wanted to chronicle our adventures and tell people about the process of quitting everything, preparing, and actually making it happen.

Once we left and started writing on our respective laptops, and all of these feelings about my father flooded out of me, I decided I needed to write my own book. It didn't have anything to do with Shannon's skills, because she is an incredible writer; I just knew that trying to blend both of our thoughts and adventures with the raw account of my father's accident and our relationship wouldn't have worked. Shannon was disappointed when I told her, but I don't regret my choice and I know she understands why I made it.

The whole booking hostels as we went thing really did work. A few days before we decided to leave each place, we would find an Internet café and research cheap hotel and hostel websites, as well as flights and trains to find the best deals. We did, of course, argue in some of those cafes. Phrases like these could be heard in our direction:

"Dude, stop looking over my shoulder."

"I found a better price!"

"What? No, I already found the best price."

"Fuck me. My time is up and I was right in the middle of filling out the reservation form. Do you have more coins?"

"It's sweltering in here. I just don't think I can take much more of this. I'm about to lose my shit. Just pick one!"

I guess we were generally tired and irritable in those sessions, which caused the occasional head-butting, but we always got through it and at least for the first half of the trip, the getting from place to place part went smoothly. I think that about covers it. Now, let's go to Australia so we can get fatter and swim with bull sharks.

CHAPTER 12

Eulogy

FIVE (SIX) POUNDS later, we said goodbye to Italy and hit the road for Sydney, Australia. The two flights from Italy to Sydney lasted twenty-one hours. My ankles swelled and I missed the smells of Tuscany. That had been my favorite place so far. I loved lounging around, writing, reading, and eating. Finding the courage to face the scary parts of my life also felt really good. I tried to leave some of my ghosts in that dusty library.

We landed in Sydney and bought tickets to our first rugby game. The Eels/Bulldogs playoff match would draw seventy-thousand people. Before the game, we spent the day wandering around the city. We traversed the enormous Sydney Harbour Bridge and recorded video of the opera house. Yes, it's gargantuan and looks like a bunch of large eggs stacked sideways. That day, we drank beers the size of small children and shopped. At sunset, we boarded a metro train and headed for the game. The second we arrived, we knew we were in for a treat.

Shannon and I skipped into the booming stadium and felt the place rumble. The experience would be nothing like watching football games back home. People with team colors painted on their faces waved flags and blew into plastic horns. The seats smelled like beer and you could cut the energy in the air with a machete. We found our spot between a kid with a giant orange team finger and a man with black stripes painted all over his cheeks.

Watching rugby live is exhilarating. The players are built like brick huts and have no qualms about bashing each other repeatedly. They cradle the ball and fly down the field with brute determination, as members of the other team beat them into the ground. The tackles never stop and the game explodes with a fever that isn't present in North American football. Fans teeter on the edge of their seats and pauses don't come often. When the offense can't make a goal in time, they kick it in the opposite direction and the game continues.

Rugby looked like more of a cross between football and wrestling to me.

As we followed the ball, people in the stands yelled, "Smawsh eem!"

In an attempt to fit in, we yelled it, too. "Smash. Him!" It didn't sound the same coming from us, so we yelled, "Blitz!"

The Eels won and went on to play in some other championship game, which they lost. I wished we could watch games like that back home. It was more exciting than football or baseball could ever be.

On our third day in Australia, Shannon and I took a ferry to North Sydney to Taronga Zoo. I knew we'd be able to pose for pictures with koalas; I just didn't know if we could hold them. I hoped that if I could hold one, it would love me so much that the zoo person would have to pull us apart like a scene out of *Annie*. Unsure, I visualized the bear/human relationship that didn't yet exist. Similar to the beginning of most relationships in my life, my expectations didn't match reality.

The koala exhibit contained several bears lounging across tree branches. They were so asleep, I thought they might roll off onto the ground. I should mention we've been told they aren't actually bears, but koalas look like bears, so I'm sticking with it.

We walked into the bear's den where a mother and baby koala slept. Both sprawled out along tree branches right next to each other. Shannon and I got to take as many pictures as we wanted, but we couldn't touch the bears. *Dang it.* It was nice to see them close up, but I wanted more. Each time we snapped a shot of the baby, it turned its head the other way with eyes closed. We figured the koalas got sick of being bothered all day. I certainly wouldn't want someone photographing me while I slept and drooled.

After moseying around Australia's capital city for about a week, we rented a car and made our way up to Surfers Paradise. We drove through rolling green hills and over enormous rushing rivers. I wondered about kangaroos, but we never found any outside the zoo.

"You know, I don't think kangaroos cruise around the land here like they do in the movies," I told Shannon.

"Yeah, I know. Where are they?"

Not an hour later, Shannon spotted about a dozen kangaroos, grazing in a field off the side of the road.

"Stooooop!" she screamed, pointing.

I hit the brakes, pulled over, and dashed out of the car so fast, I forgot to put it in park. Thankfully, Shannon noticed the car rolling and did it for me.

Experiencing a kangaroo up close was nothing like seeing it on television. They hopped around goofily and even sat on their tails. The joey in the pouch looked like a snuggly stuffed animal. They moved a little but mostly stayed put. Ecstatic to see them in their natural habitat, we stayed with the group for several minutes before the fur balls bounced away.

We drove for hours and took in the superb landscape outlining the eastern coast of Australia. It was a mixture of trees, streams, little forests, and fruit stands. We planned to stay in Surfers Paradise on the Gold Coast in Queensland, with a girl I used to babysit back home.

Cortney was now twenty-four and living the life down under. Over email, we arranged to stay with her and her roommate, Jenn, for a few days. They were both in graduate school and would be finishing up in a month. We expected they'd be in full celebration mode and we wanted to join in.

Jenn greeted us warmly when we got to their building and took us up to the apartment. Her short blond hair bobbed around radiant tanned skin. She and Cortney met on orientation day at their university and became instant best friends. Photographs of the two of them, wearing smiles and sunglasses, covered tables and shelves throughout their front room.

Fresh air blew through the windows of the tenth floor balcony. The spacious apartment looked out onto palm trees and ocean. A lone mattress sat on the living room floor for us. The idea of sleeping in a home instead of a hotel felt dreamy.

When Cortney came home, I hugged her and cried. She looked so grown up with her long blond hair, blue eyes, and gazelle-like tanned legs. Several years had passed since I'd last seen her. Since her family lived next to my father's property, and Cortney's father and mine were close, I couldn't help but make the connection. I thought about the life I'd had back when I was Cortney's babysitter.

Cortney's family had gone through a lot of the same grief mine had. For years, Cortney's father couldn't talk about my dad without getting choked up. The two of them had hunted together quite a bit. When I looked at Cortney, I thought of her playing with my little brother, Dylan.

"You look so pretty," I kept saying. "I'm just so happy to see you." What I felt like saying was, "Isn't this strange? When I knew you before, my father was alive and I got to hug my little brother all the time," but I couldn't say that. Many years had passed and everyone was supposed to be all right with it all. In those moments, I wished I was.

Cortney told us her schooling revolved around travel and event planning. She didn't know what she would do next, but she had experience working in hotels and planning events for them. I asked about her family and she told us about her little brother.

"He fell out of a tree and almost died. Didn't you know?"

"No. What happened?" I couldn't believe it. I really hadn't known. How could I? I had purposely stayed away from her family to avoid reminders of the things that hurt. They also still lived next door to my former stepmother, which made going there a little awkward and difficult.

"He was with a friend in San Diego, where he was going to college, and they were waiting for a ride. My brother was lounging in a tree and the branch broke. He fell and hit all the branches on the way down. He hit his head and broke a lot of bones. He had to move back home to recuperate. I was at the hospital with my family for a week. He keeps getting better, but it's been an uphill battle. We are so proud of him, though."

I was stunned. Here I was, swimming through my own pain and memories, and I didn't know Cortney's family had gone through something agonizing, too. It had happened about three years before; I hadn't seen them in at least five.

Cortney told me one of my dad's friends had died of alcoholism. She also told me she had run into Dylan back home and he was doing great. She said her family hardly ever saw my former stepmother. I wasn't surprised to hear that. She had remarried around a year or two after my father's death and from what I'd heard, didn't associate too much with his old friends. Cortney's stories were interesting to hear, but I felt out of the loop. I had no association anymore. I was an outsider looking in on a life that used to be mine.

I went to bed a little blue, but I was excited for the next day. Jenn and Cortney invited us to a boat party with about thirty of their friends. We loved boats and couldn't wait to explore the waters around Queensland. Would we out-age everyone on board? Most certainly, but Shannon and I didn't care; we'd experienced the same thing a dozen times so far.

Cortney and Jenn told us the boat would leave at eleven. We decided to get up at nine and take showers. To our dismay, people started arriving at nine. As I showered, Shannon stood in her pajamas, greeting youngsters in the living room. I didn't know this until I walked out with wet hair, a tee shirt, and my pajama pants on. Pale-faced, Shannon stood, holding her toothbrush, amidst five bikini-clad partygoers, already drinking mimosas and picking songs on the stereo.

"Hi, I'm Michelle," I said, reaching my hand out to one of them. I then grabbed my clothes as fast as I could and followed Shannon back into the bathroom. Not knowing whether we should laugh or cry, we quickly got ready.

"Jesus! I mean, I was just lying there on the mattress and people started walking in."

"Dude, I know. Not to mention they look about ten. I don't even want to get my fat ass in a bathing suit in front of these people. They seem nice, but they must think we are fricken' dinosaurs."

"I don't even know what to wear. Should I wear this?" Shannon held up her green sundress that she'd already worn about sixty-two times.

"Yes, wear that. We can't worry so much. This is kind of a college party, but screw it. Let's just have a good time. Why we gotta be so old?"

After we got it together, we went back into the living room where about twenty-five young people drank beers and geared up for the great boating adventure. We awkwardly introduced ourselves.

"Hi, I'm Michelle. I used to babysit Cortney."

"Hi, I'm Shannon. My friend used to babysit Cortney." Between each introduction, we pounded breakfast beers and champagne like it was all about to run out. One thing we did know was that we could out drink any of those kids, and the alcohol definitely eased our discomfort.

"Okay, let's just have fun and stick together," Shannon told me.

"Yes. Thank God we have each other (burp) because I would be dying if I was alone right now." I meant it. Thank God, Shannon was there.

Once we boarded the double-decker party boat, the sun blazed and the beer kicked in. We perched ourselves on the top deck and decompressed for the first time since we'd arrived. Shannon and I didn't even feel jealous (yeah, right) as dozens of twenty-somethings disrobed in front of us, revealing rock-hard abs and thighs smoother than patent leather. They dropped their clothes on the green AstroTurf-lined deck and posed for pictures on various iPhones.

"You know what? I'm thirty-three years old. My stomach looks like two babies wrestling and I'm not gonna worry about it," I told Shannon.

"I know. We can't. Let's cut the bullshit and stop being insecure."

As soon as the words came out of her mouth, Cortney walked up the stairs. "It's the cougars!" *You don't say?* This was definitely going to be an exercise in maintaining self-esteem.

The day unfolded and we drank more beer. Cortney eventually curled up in my lap like she was seven again and told us about boyfriends and the years I'd missed. Catching up felt good and my self-consciousness transitioned into gratitude. When people started hurling themselves off the top of the boat into the water, I confidently pulled off my sundress and leapt along with them.

"You only live once. We should do this!" I told Shannon.

"You're right. What are we doing? Since when do we care this much?"

We jumped off a dozen times, doing dives and cannon balls, hair flying through the air. That is until the record scratched.

"You guys!" someone on the boat yelled down to us. "You know there are bull sharks in that water! A lot of them!" Apparently, sharks infested those particular waterways and that's why only four of us were diving in. Terrific!

We shot like rockets to the back of the boat. I hopped up so lightning fast, my butt fell out of my bathing suit bottoms for a second. Totally over it, I laughed and put my ass back in. I practically ripped Shannon's arm out of its socket getting her up, but we were finally safe. We squinted into the water, looking for shark fins. Jaws never came.

Drunk on beer and the thrill of diving off a boat into my mid-thirties, I dreamt of sweaty palms that night.

092

I'm at my father's funeral. I wrote him a poem that I want to read, but I'm afraid. The church is so packed, people are standing outside the doors. I don't want them to hear my voice crack. I don't want them to see my tears. If I stand up and read the poem, I'm afraid I might melt in front of them, so I hand it to the pastor and he reads it for me.

I wish I could sit on your lap one last time
Just to interrupt you reading your paper
To try to make you laugh
To shift your attention to mine
I wish I could duck hunt with you for just one more day
I'd freeze my feet off and miss every duck
But be happy to be there just to hear
The funny things you'd say
I wish you could hold my hand just for one last minute
So I could feel your big fat fingers in mine
Just to be able to look up at you
Thinking you're the best dad I could get
I wish I could hug you for just one last hour

And tell you you're the best
That I listened to all you said
And learned from you
More than you'll ever know
I wish I could hear you laugh
See you smile
Kiss you goodnight
But all I can do is say farewell, my Daddy
I pray you watch out for me
Live in my heart
And be my guiding light.

I hate that poem and I love that poem. I hated my dad sometimes and I loved him, too. In Surfers Paradise, I just missed him and felt irritated. I was irritated that the dreams still haunted me and frustrated that I had to relive the experience of losing him over and over again. I wanted it all to go away.

I hustled out of the funeral as fast as I could that day. I didn't want to talk to anyone, but my dad's friends kept hugging my brothers and me, saying how awful they felt. I almost made it out before a guy who'd known my dad since childhood grabbed my arm.

"You know, he bragged about you."

"What? When?"

"All the time. He'd say, 'Did you watch the news? That's my daughter on there, really climbing the ladder.' He never stopped. He was so proud of you, Michelle."

"Then why didn't he tell me?"

The adult writing this sees a child who could not unfold her arms and say goodbye. I have compassion for that girl who missed her father so much, she didn't know what else to do but cover anguish with anger and blame.

❦

The rest of our time in Surfers Paradise, Shannon and I swam and shopped for new clothes. We made dinners with Cortney and talked about old times. We washed our clothes in their machines and couldn't believe all of our garments were clean at the same time. After a few days, we said thank you and headed north.

I left feeling like the experience had mattered. Hearing about my little brother from other people needed to stop. I wanted him to tell me the stories himself. Patience is not my virtue, though. I'd have to work on that, too.

CHAPTER 13

Exactly Where You Are

I MET TIM on the dance floor in Port Macquarie, a tiny coastal town, halfway between Sydney and the Gold Coast, on the northeastern side of Australia. We stopped there for the night after driving for about eight hours. Exhausted, Shannon and I found a pub, grabbed some beers, and took in the scenery.

A band played bluegrass while some locals danced on a wooden floor. The place smelled like pale ale and sand. We were tired, but when I discovered him, I knew I needed to hang out with Tim.

With bare feet, he danced around, letting his shoulder-length brown hair flow into his face. He snapped and smiled in his tank top and linen pants. Smitten, I got up and gently grabbed his hands. To my relief, Tim grabbed back and spun me around.

"Where ya from?" he asked.

"California. You?"

"Here. This is me mate's band. I'm also in a band. I play guitah." Oh, how I loved the guitar-playing man. At that point, I decided I would need to hear that guitar before the night was through.

Tim smelled sweaty in a good way. There's nothing better than a little man stank. His tanned skin looked shiny under the moonlight, shooting through the open doors on the side of the bar facing the beach. I studied Tim as we danced. At one point, he grabbed my hand and wrapped his other arm around my back to pull me close. His lips came within an inch of mine. "Pretty brave of ya to grab ma hands like that."

"I have a good feeling about you."

"Then I'll just have to grab onto ya for toniot."

"Grab away, my friend." Tim laughed.

He wanted to come to my hotel room, but his band mate and another friend were with him, so I went with him to stay at his band mate's house. My only condition: that he didn't kill me and promised to take me back in the morning. Tim laughed again and agreed. The band mates, Tim, and I then piled into a small van full of equipment and headed out. Tim's friends squished into the back of the car amidst guitars and sound boxes, and I got the front. We drove east, into the country.

I admit, I felt nervous, at first. "So, how far away from civilization are we actually going then?"

"Oh, about thirty more minahts." He grabbed my hand. "Don't be nervous."

"But like, where are we going, specifically?"

"Laurieton. Why? Ya been they?" He chuckled.

"No. Definitely not."

The moon shone in front of the car like a bright tunnel, pulling us in. Anything could have happened, but Tim held my hand, and for some reason, I didn't feel scared. Okay, when we got there forty-five minutes later and I found out we'd be sleeping in a shed behind his friend's mom's house, I felt a little scared.

"I live wit me mate's friend at his mum's house right now. I doin't have ah real job. We busk to mak a livin'." Tim grabbed three blankets off a shelf in the garage.

"What is busking?"

He handed me one of the blankets. "It means to ploy ya music on the street and ya get money from it."

I couldn't comprehend how Tim and his friend bought food and lived off of change in a hat. Most of all, I couldn't believe I was about to sleep in a shed.

Tim gave me some pillows to carry and told me not to worry about our sleeping arrangements. "Love Shack" rang through my noggin and I had to laugh at the situation. My mother will cringe when she reads this. I'm cringing writing it.

I've studied Buddhism. Less is more. *Let go of your attachments, Michelle.* Well, I certainly let go of my attachment to plumbing and sleeping in a solid structure that night. I walked into the shack and heard my dad's voice, "Now goddammit. Are you a goddamn dummy? What in the goddam hell are you thinking, goddammit?"

Shhhh.

Dexter would have actually thought it to be a perfect kill room. The shed could have been a set on the show. Boards and long pieces of steel hung along the walls, while sheets covered the windows. A single bed sat in the corner and a long workbench that had what looked like woodworking–person-killing–tools scattered on top of it, took up most of one side of the room. I smelled the dust and scanned the floor for mice, but didn't see any. I banked on getting creamed by mosquitoes–and possibly bludgeoned in the cranium–out there, but surprisingly, nothing happened.

Tim's guitar case leaned against an old tire in the back corner. I wanted to hear him play. I sat on the bed and leaned against the wall, pulling my knees to my chest. I wondered if the rotten wood would break behind me and I would roll right out of the structure, but I didn't.

Tim stretched out in front of me and told me about his life. I twisted his auburn hair in my fingers as he spoke. He told me he'd gotten divorced a couple of years before and he'd been sleeping in the "outside house" for months. "I just quit ma job to pursue ma music. I've dreamt about it ma whole loif and ah thought, why not now?"

As we lay in bed, listening to crickets chirping (possibly on the mattress with us), I guess I should have felt uncomfortable, but I didn't. Tim's words soothed me, and I liked hearing them.

"It's crazy, but um happy. I used to haf ah regula job, where I'd get dressed up and go to work every day. It just made ma feel so bad."

Tim and I agreed it was ridiculous to live life with one foot in the past and one in the future, a concept Eckhart Tolle explores in *The Power of Now*. Tolle says you have to do whatever you can to be in the moment and smell the flowers. It's hard to do, but when I'm in the "now" and not in yesterday or tomorrow, I am always happiest. We agreed the only place to be was here, even if here happened to be in a shed in the middle of nowhere.

The two of us talked about finding our personal legends—our purpose in life—something we'd both read about in Paulo Coelho's, *The Alchemist*.

"I think ma personal legend is playin' ma music. Ah mean, am pretty much homeless. If yad told me this is what I'd choose ten years ago, I would haf neva believed you. But hee ah am and it's the best loif. It's not like I can't get anotha job. I just want to do thas for a while."

"I think my destiny is to write. I think it starts with writing about my dad, then goes from there. I can see it all laid out. I just get scared that maybe I'm wrong."

Tim turned toward me and brushed the hair off my face. "I don't think ya wrong."

"I want to tell my story so other people who have gone through the bad stuff know we're in this together. We're all going through something. Nobody is really alone, when you think about it. It's like we are all connected, but what binds us most is our pain. It's about finding our way out of it that matters. When we can share and relate with experiences, it makes it better somehow."

"Keep writin' then. Keep troyin. Keep expressing yaself. Dat's what I'm doing. I'm not goin' to quit troyin and you shouldn't eitha." His eyes shone in the moonlight creeping through the wood slats behind me.

Tim and I talked for hours in that enchanted shack about everything we'd learned and everything we strived to be. I couldn't believe all of the same books we'd read and how much we agreed on the ideas in them. When we talked about the concept of being, we also agreed there is no "to be." We are already there.

My favorite poet is Rumi. A Persian whirling dervish, he wrote moving verses in the 13th-century. I told Tim about him, and recited some of the words in a poem called, "The Journey Starts Here."

"The real journey is right here.

The great excursion starts

From exactly where you are.

You are the world."

"I love it soy much," Tim said.

"It's good, right?"

And after wanting him to for so many minutes, he leaned in and kissed me hard. Maybe Rumi inspired him.

Tim—who is my same age—laughed out loud when I told him about the abdominal boating extravaganza.

"Cougars. She called us cougars to our faces."

We laughed again and Tim grabbed my cheeks in his hands. "Ya beautiful. Ya right where ya supposed to be. So stop worrying." *Amen.* He had given up everything and living in a shack and playing his music made him happy.

Did traveling make me happy? Was I as happy as I could be? I felt happy. I really did, when I thought about it.

I don't believe meeting Tim was a coincidence. In fact, every man I'd met on the trip so far had touched me in some way (that's what she said) and taught me something about myself. Tim proved there are sensitive men out there, who want to talk about the light inside them and the work they've done on themselves. He made me believe that people can change. He gave up a lot to wander around and pursue a dream. Similarly, I would have to live with my mother when I got back home because I had given up my apartment when I left. Tim and I weren't all that different.

We kissed some more and fell asleep in each other's arms, two human beings after the same things—happiness, contentment, and connection. I felt content that night, even though the situation was incredibly unfamiliar. I didn't think I'd be able to fall asleep in that rickety shed, but I fell off into an abyss with the crickets and God knows what else singing all around me. It was so effortless. I don't even remember falling off; I just remember waking up to Tim's gorgeous face and his hair resting on his eyes. He kissed me again and I soaked it in.

I loved listening to Tim in that strange shed. That night, it occurred to me that I could enjoy the closeness of a good man and not die at the thought of him leaving. When Tim dropped me off the next morning, I didn't miss him because I knew I wouldn't lose touch with him... and I never did.

Later that day, Shannon and I continued driving up the coast to get in a boat, headed for the Whitsunday Islands. At that point, the trip was half over and I was running low on funds. I would have to take more money out of my retirement to keep going, but I didn't care. Facing myself, the writing, and everything else was so worth it; I didn't regret one minute, one kiss, or one Australian dollar spent.

CHAPTER 14

Shooting Stars

IN HINDSIGHT, WE should have done more research before we boarded the Reef Cruiser. The company that chartered the boat scheduled to take us around the Great Barrier Reef had, apparently, been sued more than once for, among other things, leaving divers abandoned in shark-infested waters overnight. One such case had made international news the year before, but we had no idea.

Shannon and I enthusiastically booked the five-day excursion, which included scuba diving. I had watched my father scuba dive growing up and always wanted to do it myself. I hoped the experience would somehow bring me closer to him.

We were told to be at a sail shop at 7:00 PM for takeoff. As the hour approached and no one else showed up, we decided something was wrong. I ran down the street to the main office and the lady told me, "Oi! We haf been trying to get ahold of ya. You were supposed to get down to the dock, not the shop. If ya hurry, ya might still make the boat."

"You were trying to call us? On what phone? There's no phone," I told her, frustrated. I sprinted back down the street to grab Shannon and a cab. "We might be hosed. We gotta hustle."

We got in a cab and told the driver to please hurry. Okay…we were a little ruder than that. "Seriously, dude! For the love of God. Please!"

He really didn't ease our discomfort. "Youse not gonna make it," he said, three times.

"Yes, you said that. Thank you. Keep going."

We arrived and sprinted down a dock to find ten other passengers lined up by the boat. *Take that, cabdriver!*

Three people in front greeted us with clipboards. Kelsey was short, blond, and tan. She annoyed us immediately by clicking her tongue ring against her teeth as she spoke. "Nice of you (click) to make it."

We would soon find out she had two boyfriends—the other two crew members on either side of her—and they didn't know about each other. Or, at least, one thought he was her boyfriend and the other knew he was the side dude, but didn't care. All of them grossed me out from the second I met them.

Alejandro, the real boyfriend, looked as though he had just woken up. Pieces of his brown hair slanted straight up over the top of his head. He wore dirty board shorts and didn't look us in the eye when he spoke. I didn't know if he was stoned or tired, but he came across as a really strange cat.

Desmond, the secret boyfriend, was a clean-cut brunette from Massachusetts, who knew everything about everything. He'd head off on a tangent and talk non-stop about the best this and the best that. Sometimes, he'd be rambling on about something and we'd just walk away, tired of listening to him run his mouth. Each time, we could still hear him talking as we rounded the corner.

Shannon did the perfect impression of him. "Well, Michelle. I am not just a diver. I'm a dive *master*, just so you know," she'd say, darting her eyes back and forth. "New England marijuana is by *far* better than California marijuana. Just ask anyone."

Once all twelve of us boarded, we found our room and discovered that one of two toilets on our side of the boat was broken, and three girls in the room next to us would have to share our miniature bathroom. On top of that, the broken toilet sloshed out some of the foulest smelling funk you could ever imagine. The boat rocked and a trail of ass-stench flowed into our room like stinky smoke that made our eyes burn. We couldn't escape it and wondered how we would be able to sleep through the smell.

"Hey, Desmond. Is that smell going to be like that all night?" I asked our first night.

"Oh, no. No worries. I will spray some eucalyptus oil on it before we go to bed and it'll smell just fine after that. Tip-top shape!"

Really? It smelled so bad, I didn't think anything could mask it.

"Desmond, why didn't someone fix this thing before we left?" Shannon asked.

"Ohhh, well. They tried, but they will just have to do it when we get back." Good thing we were getting our money's worth...

Desmond sprayed eucalyptus oil on the poop and the smell changed from feces, to feces with mint on top. Our eyes and noses burned from shit *and* eucalyptus and we were forced to sleep in that soupy air for four nights. The stench was putrid and we both woke up nauseated.

The next morning, we bobbed and weaved up to breakfast to find Desmond, rushing everyone out into a raft for a day trip to some gorgeous beaches nearby. Desmond was irritated people weren't moving fast enough. "Come on! Lightning speed!" It was like we were little kids being hounded by a babysitter. Despite the rush, getting to those beaches ruled; they were some of the most beautiful we'd ever seen. White sand blanketed the shores of Whitehaven Beach, on Whitsunday Island, as greenish-blue translucent water splashed around for miles. Our guides told us to wear stinger suits to protect us from poisonous jellyfish, but we didn't listen. The water felt too good on our skin, so we took the risk.

We lay in the sand and absorbed the heat from the sun as people from other tour boats frolicked around us. Basking on that beach made us feel like we were inside of a postcard, but like a bad dream, Desmond returned an hour later to take us back.

"Okay. Chop, chop. We got some eggs and Canadian bacon ready for you."

Unfortunately, the smell had intensified back on the boat and our hosts got more annoying. Kelsey suggested we all play a game where we describe our favorite sexual positions.

Now, I'm not a prude (obviously), but I didn't care to talk about my bedroom skills around those dipsticks, so I listened and laughed when Kelsey got a volunteer to mime her favorite position. *Like doggy style was something innovative.*

Later that night, I asked Alejandro about the jellyfish and the stinger suits. "Hey, Alejandro. You guys never told us about the stinger suits and why we should wear them in the water. Can you tell me what to look out for?"

He stared into space. "Some jellyfish. Clear ones."

I'm not joking. That's exactly what he said. "Yeah, I know. You mentioned that. What kind are bad? What do they look like?"

"Oh, most are really small." His grain-of-sand answers felt like paper cuts.

"No, seriously. Can I see them at all?"

"Some, but most are small." Mind you, each time he responded, he looked out into the sky again, like he was on mushrooms. Maybe he was.

"Alejandro, how would I know if I've been bitten by the bad kind and not just a regular jellyfish? Please clarify."

"Oh, you get nauseous. And you are in pain. A lot of the time, you die." It was like we were in an episode of *Star Trek: The Next Generation* and Alejandro was the emotionless android character, Data. *Blatant Star Trek plug.* Although, that's not even true; Data would have gotten right to the truth.

Through our conversation, I learned I couldn't avoid the most dangerous jellyfish because they were too small to see. Great. I also got double confirmation that Alejandro was a total space cadet.

Scuba diving with Alejandro and the other crewmembers was a difficult decision to make because we had never done it before, and we would be putting our lives in the hands of idiots. We decided to do it (because we were on a boat in the Great Barrier Reef) and found out Alejandro would be our guide. How could this be possible? How did that guy even make it through the training? Would he float away into attention–deficit-land while we were underwater?

Alejandro gave us stinger suits and dictated a quick lesson on breathing with the mouth thing. Terror surged through me as I recalled a *Dateline* special where some asshole pulled that thing out of his wife's mouth underwater and drowned her. See, I don't even know the name of the breather thing. We were so unprepared. I knew the five-minute-long tutorial was not enough. An avid diver, my father always stressed the importance of following meticulous safety rules. Knowing I'd be risking my life, I accepted my choice to dive anyway.

Alejandro harnessed the tanks on our backs and threw us into the water. I'm not kidding. It all went that fast. For those who had never scuba dived before (us), it was a terrifying thing. Imagine having forty pounds of gear on—including a weight belt—and falling "back first" into the ocean. Our first instinct was to fight our way back to the surface to avoid being dragged to the bottom. The good news was we had vests full of air on, which kept us on the surface. I panicked when I splashed in, but thankfully, I didn't sink.

After we got settled in the water, we crept down a rope tied to an anchor on the seafloor. Alejandro led and we followed. We were supposed to clear our ears as we went down, which is not an easy task. My ears had a terrible time clearing. I wiggled my jaw and plugged my nose. Each time I went down further, I prayed my ears would adjust, but the ocean kept pressing harder into my head.

I could hear my father telling me, "You can do this. This is the goddamned Great Barrier Reef, for Christ's sake!" *I know, Dad, but I'm scared.* Or maybe he was saying, "You moron! What idiot is scuba diving with no training?"

After watching me struggle for a few minutes, Alejandro pulled me up to the surface and told me he didn't think I should continue. Maybe he wasn't as dumb as I thought.

"I can do this. I'm trying again. I'm fine." I was more determined than ever to make it work, but I didn't want to injure myself... *or die.* I also felt nervous breathing through the breather thing. I shouldn't have been scuba diving in the first place, but vowed one more time to make it work. Praying, I kicked back down the rope.

By the grace of God, my ears cleared. Each time I went down, I pushed the air out, holding my nose. I heard the longest sqeeeeeeeeeak. *What a relief.* Once I loosened up, I felt incredibly blessed to be there.

Diving in the reef is PHENOMENAL. Red, blue, and florescent pink coral crept and crawled along the seafloor like brains, antlers, and shapes I couldn't even imagine. The coral also made a crackling sound, which was fascinating. I was so relieved I had figured the ears out, because once we got down there, the experience moved me.

Shannon and I laughed underwater because Alejandro ended up grabbing each of us by the back. Afraid we'd float away, he held Shannon on the left and me on the right, pulling us along like floating children. That made the dive easier because all I had to do was breathe and float. The breathing did continue to frighten me, though. The whole time, I worried I was breathing wrong or that something would malfunction and I wouldn't be able to get back up to the top. I had to constantly talk myself out of that fear.

As we floated, I transported back to the last time I had worn a wetsuit. I was fourteen and my father and I were in Tomales Bay in Northern California. An avid abalone diver, he had asked if I wanted to go with him and I bit. Someone had given him an old suit that turned out to be a woman's cut, so it fit me perfectly. We set out and my dad told me what to do.

"Hold your breath and when you spot an abalone, pry it off the rocks with this little shovel. I'll give you a weight belt and it'll help you get down there."

Unfortunately, the weight belt was so light, every time I went down, I bounced back up to the surface. I could never make it to the seafloor, no matter how hard I tried.

"Dad!" I screamed. My dad had just popped up to the surface, abalone shell in hand. "What the heck? I can't stay down there."

"Sorry, honey. I don't think I made that weight belt heavy enough. I didn't want you to sink. Just let me go down a couple more times and we'll be done. If you get cold, just pee in the wetsuit and it'll warm you up."

"I thought I wasn't supposed to pee in it."

"Well, you aren't. But who's going to know? It will be our secret."

With that, he tilted his head toward the sky and took a deep breath. "DON'T PEE IN THE WETSUIT, HONEY!" Other divers bobbing nearby turned to look at us. "IT'S VERY BAD FORM, SO WE DON'T DO IT!"

"YES, FATHER!" I shouted back, laughing.

He winked at me and disappeared again.

I floated around in awe of my dad as he bounced up and down with shell after shell in hand. He was so adventurous. I felt close to and loved by him that day because I stopped to appreciate the uniqueness of my silly father. I wish I could go backward to slow down and absorb more of those irreplaceable moments.

Our Great Barrier Reef dive lasted for about an hour (one of the coolest hours of my life). I'm so glad I tried it, but I will never dive again until I take lessons and figure out what the hell I'm doing first.

We had other fun moments, too. Some nights, Shannon and I would lie on top of the boat and yell, "Michelle's dad! Give us a shooting star!"

Shannon would also ask her grandpa and her friend, Brian, who had died of cancer the year before, to send us some stars. The shooting stars would always come, too. They'd fly across the night sky in a show just for us.

Nights like that made me believe in everything. They were enchanting and made me feel like my father was there. Some stars shot forever and some we could only catch out of the corners of our eyes. We listened to the boat, rocking back and forth, as the water lapped the sides in a slow clap. The motion calmed us. My sweet friend and I didn't have a care in the world, and although we knew it couldn't be like that forever, we basked in those starry nights.

Our last day on the boat, we all watched the movie, *Australia*. I thought I had seen it twenty years before when it was released as *Far and Away*, but *Far and Away* was actually good. *Australia* seemed fitting for the situation though. Shannon and I ended up sleeping out in the dining room that night because the shit smell was finally too intense for us to take. We woke up to people eating cereal beside us and shook our heads at our latest ridiculous endeavor.

When we got back into town, the two of us and five other passengers found the boat company's corporate office and complained about the sewage problem. We were told we'd get a refund, but we didn't hear anything for weeks. A month later, the company sent a note that said they would send us a $50 check. We never got it and at that point, we didn't care. All stink aside, the boat trip gave us some fun memories and a lot of material for Chapter 14.

CHAPTER 15

Love of My Life

WE LEFT AUSTRALIA, hot and sticky, wearing tank tops and flip-flops. When we landed in Christchurch, on the southern island of New Zealand, our arms almost froze off. New Zealand was heading out of its winter and temperatures had dipped to near freezing in some places. I'd developed a bad chest cold, and all I wanted to do was sleep. We were hungry though, so we ended up going out for Indian food and wine instead. I figured sleep could wait for Tikka Masala.

"I know I'm ready to be in love, married, and all of it when I get back. I've never been so sure in my life," Shannon told me, ripping a piece of Naan bread. "I just keep thinking about it. All of the people we're meeting are great, but I know what I want and I don't need to meet anyone else to figure that out."

"I'm getting clearer on the whole thing, as well." A waiter walked by. "Excuse me. Can you please bring me some more hot sauce?" I turned to Shannon. "I can't taste for shit. My nose is so stuffed."

"You know what's interesting? How simple it all is. You and I get along best when we help each other. Do you realize that?" Shannon asked.

I did. "That's the secret, I think. It's so important to look out for your person."

The cold kicked my ass in the days that followed. Temperatures dipped outside and I couldn't get warm on the inside. Each day, Shannon asked me what I needed before she went out. She brought me cough drops, Kleenexes, and these little candies I liked. It was so simple. The act of helping each other gave us something to ponder. Reaching out to one another made our ship sail smoother. If I'd understood that more in my past relationships, I believe they could've been better. Instead of trying to win, I think I could have been more in tune with what my partner needed. Whether it was to listen or to give him space, I could have been different.

Tiny Elvis and I slept for a couple of days. While I'm certain he dreamt about growing to "real man size," I thought about the men I'd met on the trip. I thought about Costa Rica Charlie, telling me to face my fears and Italy Hugh and I trying to survive the ghost attack. I realized that most men aren't that different around the world. Some are captivating; some are not. Some reminded me of Antonio Banderas and some happily danced around barefooted and slept in sheds. None of that mattered. What mattered was it started and ended with me. It wasn't about how they acted. It was about who *I* allowed into my life, how I treated that person, and how I treated myself inside of a relationship. It was about knowing there are great guys everywhere and I was the one who had the power to let one in… one who wanted to be there.

After Myles and I broke up, I avoided dating for a long time so I didn't have to go through the pain of a breakup again. I didn't want to do that anymore. I'd have to be brave and open myself up to vulnerability, possibly for the first time ever. It's not surprising I sidestepped closeness and intimacy. When loss sticks to you like a Siamese twin, it's easy to find ways to keep it from happening again.

In my cold medicine haze, I thought about my little brother. I dreamt I saw Dylan, walking down the street toward me. We were allowed to be in each other's lives again. I woke up wishing the dream was real. When I went down to the coffee shop to get some tea and check my email, I could see that Dylan was online, so I instant messaged him. I'd never done that before for fear of scaring him off, but at that moment, I didn't care. *What do I have to lose?*

What's up? I wrote

When Dylan wrote right back, I almost choked on my chamomile.

Hey, Sister. How are you?

I'm good. I'm in Australia. I held my breath, waiting for his answer. Thankfully, it came. We chatted online for several minutes; it was the most communication we'd had since my father died. He told me about his girlfriend of five years. He said he really loved her. He also said he enjoyed college in Southern California and that he lived with a couple of guys.

I wanted to cry during that message exchange because he reiterated his desire to catch up in person. I desperately wanted that to happen, but he had said that before and he'd never come through. This time, he gave me his phone number and said he was serious.

I wanted to throw my arms around my little brother and hear everything he wanted to tell me. With each word he wrote, I imagined him in the car, holding up toys and making faces to make me laugh. Then, my mind went to a vision of him standing in the darkness on the driveway when I had come home the night our dad died. I wished I'd been right when I told him we'd always be together.

I couldn't wait to see him. Thinking about it made me nervous. I hoped I wouldn't cry too hard and make an ass of myself. Having his phone number gave me something tangible to focus on, for once.

Once I recovered, Shannon and I took an eight-hour bus ride down to Queenstown. We'd heard from more than one person that Queenstown was the place to go on the South Island. We got there and saw a lake surrounding a picturesque area with enormous snowcapped mountains towering above it. Queenstown took my breath away. Posters plastered all over store windows advertised adventure sport trips galore, so we booked a boat excursion for the next day.

Our jet boat and kayaking day kicked off in the changing room where our tour guides told us to pick fleece sweaters out of a box. We would bundle the fleece over scuba suits and boots. The fleeces, mind you, were straight from the nineties and we laughed as we put them on. They were pink and purple with paisley patterns and stars. All that was missing were scrunchies.

I pulled my bright pink and purple fleece on. "Do I look like Tiffany?"

"Dude, you're straight up Deborah Gibson."

I slipped my hand through a solo black glove with several holes in it. "Look at me. Cuz this is thrillaaaaaaa," I sang.

What a sight. Here we were, wearing sleeveless scuba suits, snowflake-covered beanies, and scuba shoes with nineties fleece over them. Shannon's gloves even had pink flowers on them. As we stood in the changing room, snapping pictures of ourselves with toes in the air and a holey glove in front of my face, I knew it would be a ridiculous day. We got blue jackets to wear over the fleeces and we were off.

The jet boat whipped us around and through minuscule stretches of river that seemed so shallow, it was amazing we were able to make it across. Our driver told us the boat could glide over four inches of water; he wasn't kidding. We zipped and spun around in circles until the icy river splashed our faces. Snowy mountains towered above us, reflecting in every ripple. Sometimes, the wind blew the snow out into the air like frozen powdered sugar on our cheeks.

They'd filmed *The Lord of the Rings* on the mountain ranges above us. I imagined the actors, sword-fighting on them. I could also see the hobbits in my mind, cruising around on their journeys along the banks of the river. The sun shone on our faces and the wind burned, but it didn't matter. I felt free. The future presented itself as we glided across shallow water, open and fresh. *It can be wonderful again.*

After we finished boating, we stopped on the shore to receive a kayaking lesson.

"Ya need to do one row in a half circle and not a straight line. Theen ya need to use the peeddle as a rudda," our instructor barked. He was very committed to kayaking and I could tell he really wanted us to understand his instructions.

Unfortunately, I could comprehend about seventy percent of his accent. Most of his instructions went in one ear and out the other. I wasn't paying attention because I was trying to remember the names of those two little baby hobbits that were like twins or something. Were they hobbits or little elves? I do know one of them ended up playing Charlie on *Lost*.

"Now, leesten. If ya don't leesten, ya may as well just know ya kayak could fleep." The guy talked a lot.

How could kayaking be so difficult? I just thought we'd figure it out as we went. I was nervous that, if we messed it up, we'd get in trouble, but I still didn't listen. I wished I could have played a part in *The Lord of the Rings*. That movie was so long.

I snapped out of my daydream in time to blow up our kayak. It was actually called a "Funyak" and we had to pump an air thing to fill it up. I asked our instructor if we had to blow the bottom up, too, because it seemed like it already had air in it and he got me good.

"Well, yees! It isn't going to fill eet-silf up."

Jerk.

When we got in the boat, I volunteered to be the back of the boat steering girl. "I really think I can do this. I have a bit of boating experience," I told Shannon. When I think about it now, I realize how stupid that was because I have zero experience steering a kayak, let alone a Funyak. I know how to float on an inner tube down a river in Chico, California, and I know how to body surf. *Do those count?*

We got in the kayak and all of four seconds passed before the thing started hauling ass through the current. Both of us took turns stabbing our oars in the water on opposite sides of the boat.

"Shit! I may have taken on this role of boat captain prematurely, Shan. I'm scared!"

The river jerked the Funyak around a corner.

"Which way do we paddle?" Shannon yelled.

"Wait, I don't know. Wait!" The boat shot through a narrow channel. Water rushed and the kayak shuddered and shook.

"What should we do?" Shannon yelled again.

We tipped sideways in the rushing water. All I could think about was how embarrassing it would be if we flipped in the first thirty seconds. By the grace of God, the Funyak corrected itself right before one of the instructors jumped into the water and pulled us down to calmer streams. Embarrassed, we laughed our heads off after we passed her. It turned out, Shannon hadn't listened to the demo, either.

The rest of the day consisted of us paddling wrong and rolling down the river backward most of the time. We laughed and laughed as the instructor told us we weren't "doing it right." Sometimes, when the water got shallow, we had to get out and pull the boat through rocks. We were sweating like pigs in those wetsuits.

Shannon and I pushed our oars through the water and watched glaciers unfold in front of us. Every picture I took out there could've been a painting. Sometimes, the water quit rushing and sound stopped. I inhaled the clean air.

When we stopped on the shore for lunch, they had soup, sandwiches, and all sorts of food laid out for us. Shannon and I gobbled it down, letting our wetsuits dry in the sunshine. When we finished eating, we marched back to the kayaks while performing every exercise pose we could think of. With feet sloshing in my boots, I did squats as Shannon lifted a branch above her head like it was a huge dumbbell. We looked so stupid in those wetsuits. We laughed so hard, one of the women in the group said, "Boy, what did they put in your soup?"

I'm not sure what made everything so funny that day. Maybe it was the sun or all the scenery. *Oh, the Funyak. It had to have been the Funyak.*

On our final stretch, we did one last spin and Shannon made the best suggestion of the day. "Let's roll it in backward and piss him off one last time."

So we turned our boat the wrong way and paddled in. The Funyak skidded against the shore and we howled so hard, I worried we'd get caught in the current and be swept back down the river. We got the backward boat to stick, though, and we were safe. You should have seen the main instructor guy's face when we came in back first. He wasn't smiling.

We stopped at a possum fur shop on the way home and learned that possums are pests, so New Zealanders are encouraged to kill them. They hate possums because possums eat too many endangered plants. Get a New Zealander talking about possums and they won't shut up.

Staring at myself in the mirror with a possum fur hat on my head, I thought of the vegans back home in San Francisco. They would've lost it, seeing someone wearing a possum fur hat for real. I smirked and bought my mom some possum gloves.

There was a light at the end of the darkness my father and I had created after our bloody nose fight. As I lay in bed after kayaking, I thought about sitting at my boyfriend's parent's house, wondering what to do next.

I thank God I had the motivation at eighteen to still go away to college after I moved out of my father's house. It was summertime, and I was set to leave in a few months. Before the fight, my father had agreed to pay for my tuition. For several weeks after our throw down, I wondered if I should stay back with my boyfriend and continue taking classes at the community college.

After vivid images of being barefoot and pregnant at eighteen sped through my mind, I decided I had to go away to school, so I could become more than a wife and mother. Becoming a wife and mother meant everything to me; I just wanted to go to school and experience a little bit of the world before I settled down. It took all of my courage to go back out to our property and ask my father if he would still pay for my education.

My hands shook and my heart pounded as I drove down the long driveway to the house. I could see my father out in the field and I headed toward him.

Don't cry, Michelle. Don't cry. I missed him so much. I wanted him to miss me, too.

I got out of the car and walked into the field where he sat on the tractor, staring at me. He shut the motor down, pulled off his gloves, and slouched over the steering wheel in silence.

Terrified, I explained that I still wanted to go to college. I kept it simple and tried to think happy thoughts, so he wouldn't sense my pain. Standing there, I wished I could run to him so he could hold me and erase the hurt. "So, yeah. I'm sorry about our fight. I'm sorry I left like that. I wanted to know if you still would pay—"

"Yes." What I'm pretty sure he wanted to say was, "Please get out of that situation and go make something of yourself."

"Thank you so much. I won't let you down."

I left for Chico State a few months later, but not before my father and I started to mend our broken relationship. It happened on a camping trip that summer. My boyfriend and I joined a bunch of other family friends, my father, and my little brother on a fishing trip in Tomales Bay. We all brought trailers and tents and set up along the foggy beach near Point Reyes. It was the weekend before I left for college and I looked forward to seeing my dad. I'd seen him a couple of times after our fight, but our relationship was still incredibly strained.

Those fishing trips were the best because we fished, dove for abalone, clammed, and caught crabs in cages before cooking it all around our campfire at night. Our crew loved to eat, drink, and tell stories, all bundled up in the crisp, salty air. After he put my little brother to bed one night, my dad sat next to me on a bench by the fire and opened up.

"These last few months have been so hard on me, honey. I can't eat or sleep. I'm so worried about you. I don't like not having you around."

The words shocked me and stuck like honey to my soul. They were the nicest words my dad had ever said to me and I actually held my breath when he said them. He did care. It had mattered to him that I left.

"You are the love of my life. I just wanted you home."

I could've lived and died on that bench. My dad had never used the word "love" before. He loved me and I felt whole, for once.

The heat from the campfire burned my face. I wanted to scoot back from the fire pit, but my dad had his enormous arm around me and I felt safe with my head buried in his chest, so I didn't budge. Nothing could make me move. Nothing could come between us. I never wanted to be anywhere else. As the flames crackled, my dad and I drank beer and caught up on the months we'd missed.

"You should see my dorm room. It's like a closet…"

"So, here's your little brother, ass up, with his face in the mud…."

"I'm registered for five classes. Are you sure I have to take five at once?"

"So the dog swims out to get the duck in the water and it's still alive and it bites him in the mouth!"

We listened to each other long after everyone else had gone to bed. That conversation brought me so much closer to my dad and it made leaving for college a lot easier.

These beautiful parts of our relationship existed. A lot of good existed between us, too.

CHAPTER 16

❦

Brave Girl

AFTER A LOT of discussion, Shannon and I decided to do a tandem bungee jump off a bridge in Queenstown. I'd always wanted to jump over a river. There were lots of places back home where we could jump over concrete, but that didn't appeal to me. I had to talk Shannon into it, because when I examined the bridge, wedged in a canyon between two mountains, I knew I couldn't jump alone. She didn't want to miss out, so she agreed.

Bungee scared me more than almost anything. We planned to jump about 137-feet off the bridge where commercial jumping started back in the eighties. For me, the leap symbolized overcoming fears. If I got through it, it would mean I could truly do anything. I envisioned myself falling and letting go of everything that hurt. I thought so much about what I wanted to let go of and said the words in my head to make them stick.

I will let go of all the pain of that day back in October of 2000. I will also release every loss and heartbreak I've experienced since then. I will stop missing Dylan and accept that I will see him again someday. I will also fall into the reality of a new life when I get home. Everything will be all right. I will finish my Master's degree and teach. I will love with all my heart and I will get married to an amazing man and raise amazing children, who will be encouraged not to follow foreign men into love shacks in the Australian woods. I will be happy and I will wrap my arms around it all.

If only it were that easy.

The sight of people jumping off the Kawarau Bridge made me shiver. The scene was breathtaking, but it was chilling to watch daredevils dangle over the rushing river below.

My heart pounded uncontrollably on the walk out. I looked back and saw a crowd, gathered on the land beside the bridge. I wanted to run, but I knew we couldn't flake because we were in too deep and neither one of us were quitters. I didn't want to die and I sort of thought I might.

Shannon and I had to duck under a metal bar and sit on a seat so a guy could put all of our safety equipment on. They wrapped ropes and cloths around our ankles and clicked these little chains together to keep everything in place. Each jumper was also given a number. I got thirty-three and Shannon got thirty-two. When the guy said, "Thirty-three and thirty-two," I thought he was making some determination of where the ropes should go, based on our age.

"Why is it based on our age?" I asked.

"It's not. Those are just ya numbass in the lineup."

Spooky. We took that as a good omen.

The guys put harnesses around our butts and our waists so we were conjoined, checked our ankle wraps one more time, and had us inch out onto the plank.

Short of breath, I told the guy to wait. "I'm just going to need one more second here."

He didn't listen. He told us to extend our outside arms like we were flying and wrap our inside arms around each other.

I was sure the rope would snap or one of us would slip out of the harness. I also thought, at some point, with all the bouncing, we would bang into each other. Before I could protest any more, he gave us a gentle shove and we flew out into nothing. Wind punched my face. *Baby Jesus, help ussssss!*

༶

I'm standing on the curb at the airport in Sacramento, saying goodbye to my father. I'm twenty-two years old. Seven-year-old Dylan is holding on to my waist.

"Whelp, I guess your big brother is all married now. Can't believe he finally did it," Dad says.

"I can't believe I have to go back to Idaho now. How did the wedding weekend extravaganza go by so fast?" My chin quivers and I feel the tears on my cheeks.

My dad grabs my face with both hands. He wipes a tear with his big thumb. "You're my brave girl. You know that? I still cannot believe you packed up and moved there to work at that tiny little news station. Are you sure that place is even on the air?"

We laugh. I feel safe, lost in his brown eyes. "But I miss everybody. I know it's what I want and I have to start at the bottom, but sometimes I feel like I'm floating alone. I don't know if I'm doing the right thing."

My dad grabs my shoulders and looks into my eyes. "You're my brave girl. You're doing the right thing because you are strong and you wanted this. You're strong, like me, because you're mine. Now, go back there and get good so you can come back and I can watch you on TV here." He pulls me close.

I have one arm around him and the other around my little brother, who is sobbing into my thigh. I want to take them with me. I don't want to get back on the plane, but I do. I can't let my dad down.

⚭

The bungee jump skipped by in slow motion. Failing to follow the instructions to let my arm open out like a bird's wing, I hugged my stomach and tucked my head into my neck. Overcome with terror, I think I tried to crawl into my own skin. Shannon screamed, but I couldn't. Instead, a little high-pitched yeep sound came out. On replay, it sounded like whimpering.

At one point, I tried to curl into the fetal position, but the ropes wouldn't let me. When we bounced and didn't crush each other, I opened my eyes and realized I hadn't died. It was spectacular to recoil and live through it. I appreciated that part and felt relieved the bouncing would end soon.

We jiggled up and down and I tried to take it in. Our hair was supposed to touch the water in the river below, but it never did. The sky, rocks, and water blurred together. Then it hit me. Hanging upside down, with blood rushing to my head, it occurred to me that my dad had been proud of me the whole time. He never said it the way I'd wanted him to, but he adored me. He couldn't believe I moved to Idaho because it *was* brave and strong. The thought surprised me.

"Huh," I said out loud. My dad believed in me. Why was it so hard to focus on the positive when it came to my parents?

"That was sweeeeeet!" Shannon yelled.

"I knowwwwwwww!" I screamed back.

We stopped bouncing and noticed two people in a little raft, waiting to pick us up in the rushing water below. To get down, we had to grab on to a pole and be pulled into the raft. That part is fuzzy because I was still in shock. Shannon, thankfully, took charge and grabbed the pole to get us into the boat. Right as we dropped down, the raft people unhooked our ankles and told us to look up and smile at a surveillance camera on the bridge.

The sun blinded me as I searched for the camera. I needed a minute so I closed my eyes and gave up. That picture turned out hilarious. I'm lying on my back in the boat with my face all crunched up like I'm in pain. Shannon is beside me, beaming and radiant.

We laughed for days at all the images the cameras caught of the whole jumping extravaganza. They were funny because they told the story of exactly what went down in those moments.

In the first picture, we are standing on the plank with elated smiles. In the next, we're looking out on the water, blank-faced. Then, in the photos that captured the actual jump, Shannon has her arm bursting out in the air and I look like a hyperventilating baby, curled into a half-caterpillar ball next to her. Our juxtaposition was hysterical. She was straight and I was a half-moon with butt aimed high. Again, thank God, Shannon was there because I couldn't have done it without her.

I wish I could say I let go of all my pain during the jump, but I can't. Just getting through the free-fall without having a stroke had been incredibly difficult. Prayers to the baby Jesus included: *Please don't die. Please don't shit my pants. Please don't die.*

It would be nice if we could jump off a bridge and *poof*, all pain goes away, forgiveness blossoms, and catharsis occurs, but it doesn't work that way. Pain goes away, little by little, at its own pace. We can go to therapy, participate in life-threatening adventure sports, read books, or quit our jobs to travel, but pain still follows. It stays and leaves on its own terms and it doesn't care how hard we try to rid ourselves of it. All we can do is keep trying our best to sift through it, sit with it, ask it nicely to leave or, perhaps, scream at it to leave.

Pain is like a puppy, crying in a box in the garage at night. You can put a pillow over your head, but the whimpering seeps through. That dog's not going to shut up until you let it sleep with you a few nights, and then over time, it matures and doesn't bug you anymore.

Ironically, the second we got out of the little raft and back onto solid ground, Shannon suggested we go down the road and take a ride on the world's highest canyon swing. Although my fear on the bungee almost killed me, I was full of adrenaline, too, and just wanted the chance to do it all over again with my eyes open, so I agreed.

After we paid another hundred bucks, we took a van to the swing that stretched so far, it covered an entire canyon. We'd seen videos of it. I thought the swing was like this thing you sit on and it shoots you forward on a line that dips a little. When we got to the swing, I realized I was wrong.

First, we had to traverse a tiny metal bridge. It was so thin, it swayed in the wind. We grasped the railings of the world's thinnest catwalk and made it safely to yet another plank. As if the bridge wasn't terrifying enough, Shannon and I ducked down into a little box/platform thing where they would harness us up. We concluded it absolutely trumped the bungee.

Shivering, we watched the swing operator harness two people on a line and push a button that moved them out. Their feet dangled over the canyon as they swayed in the wind. The canyon swooped down so deep, we could hardly see the stream running through the bottom of it. Watching the people hang was enough to make me want to cry... again. We agreed this would be a thousand times worse than the bungee, because after they dropped us, we would free fall, then shoot across the canyon, swinging back and forth on the line.

"We have to do it. We're already here," I whispered.

"I know. This sucks."

When it was our turn, we reluctantly sat down in the swing, they cinched us in, clicked some chain links together, and pushed us out on the line.

"Are you sure everything is tight enough?" I asked the guy.

"Ya fine." He pushed a button and moved us farther out. Suspended over the canyon, I had to take deep breaths to avoid fainting. Again, I was terrified, and to make matters worse, the wind blew us around like a pinecone dangling from a branch.

Could we blow right off the line?

The guy asked us to smile for this little camera by his head and the second we turned our domes, the swing dropped so fast, our hair blew up into the place we used to be and stayed there, suspended for a few seconds before we vanished.

To my surprise, the free fall was not as paralyzing as the bungee. It didn't seem to last as long and before we knew it, we were flying out over the canyon.

What a rush.

We flew, and flew, and flew, forward across the canyon and over the stream below. It reminded me of a zip line. I heard the wind and the zipping sound. I don't think we even screamed.

When we got to the end of the rope, the swing whipped us back and forth, sometimes twisting us around and back. Closing my eyes, I imagined we were on a roller coaster. Powerful gusts blew us above the rocks and water below, adding to the intensity of the thrill.

After swinging for about two minutes at the end of the line, the operator slowly pulled us back so we could step backward onto the platform again. That was almost scarier than coming off it. We eventually found the ledge with our heels and stood up so he could unhook us. Then, Shannon and I carefully tiptoed back over the bridge. I couldn't wait to set foot on solid ground. What a relief to step off that bridge and feel the stillness of the earth below my feet.

We dedicated that day to adrenaline. We will forever call it, "Adrenaline Day." Oh, and for the record, I hope to never in my life do either of those things again.

CHAPTER 17

Meat Pies

I SPOTTED PATRICK at a tavern that sits on the harbor in Queenstown. He re-minded me a lot of Myles, with his hazel eyes, short beard, and slicked back black hair.

Shannon and I had planned to stay in Queenstown for only a couple days, but we extended our visit several times over. That place was so spell-binding, with its glaciers and charismatic art and restaurants all sprawled about. There was a jazz festival going on while we were there, and various bands played around us throughout the day and night. We just couldn't leave, so we didn't.

Patrick—who was my age—worked as a server at the tavern. I followed him with my eyes as I drank beers with Shannon. He had a mysterious way about him as he stood, quietly monitoring the room. I liked Patrick's linebacker shoul-ders and muscular arms. I wanted to hear his voice (suck face), so I went for it.

When Patrick's co-worker walked by, I grabbed him and pointed to the man I wanted to meet.

"What's his name?" I shouted over the loud music.

"Deereek."

"Ask him what time he gets off because I want to have a drink with him."

Five minutes later, Patrick walked up. "Ya want to heef a drink?"

"Yep!"

"Wait for me. I'll be done in a heef-owa."

"Okay, Derek!"

"It's Peetreek."

Oops. I couldn't hear in there.

Shannon and I waited, but got impatient after forty-five minutes and told Patrick we would meet him at another bar. He told us to give him five more minutes and I'm glad we did. I can't believe I almost left.

Patrick took us to another packed bar where he introduced Shannon to his friend, Shane. The four of us hit it off, laughed, talked, and drank. There weren't enough chairs available so I plopped down into Patrick's lap. His arms felt like a seatbelt around my waist.

"Ameerican gal. Ya pretty cute, ya know?"

I rested my head on his shoulder. "Can you say that a million times tonight?"

"Can I have ya longah than tonight?"

"Why, yes. Maybe you can."

Patrick and I fell into warm fuzzy-ville after five minutes, so I decided not to leave him for three days. Our two nights in Queenstown had now morphed into ten.

Patrick lived with a roommate outside of town. The second I got to his house, I made him my temporary boyfriend in my head. We hid in his wing of the house and boned so very many times and for once (for the love of GOD), I enjoyed it. He knew what he was doing, too, which was a double bonus. I felt elated and beautiful, and Patrick couldn't keep his hands off me. For some reason, I quit worrying about my body, his body, my not knowing him, and everything else I regularly obsessed about.

For days, we lay in bed, laughing and goofing off. We played Halo on the Xbox, and he taught me how to shoot aliens and other bad guys with precision.

"Aim ya gun and hide behind the car at the seem time!"

"I know! I'm trying!" I giggled, fighting off his advances mid-game.

Patrick pulled me back into an ocean of sheets, soft skin, bedhead, and the closeness of a (pretend) relationship, over and over. It had been so long since I had let myself go there. My New Zealander brute and I continued to curl our bodies around each other and held on tight.

He told me about growing up on the South Island. He worked at a car wash during the week and served on the weekends. His life was simple and he liked it that way. "I can't believe how comfortable I am wit ya, and I've only known ya for a dee."

"Me, too." *God, he looked like Myles.*

Patrick took me out for my first meat pie experience. Those things are all the rage in New Zealand. People there eat little pies full of meat the way Americans down Starbucks coffee. They're everywhere and as I found out, the pies are divine. I ate one that had chicken in it and another filled with lamb and mint. They were hot and so home cooked; the pies made me all warm and ready to get back in bed with Patrick.

So I did.

My fake boyfriend showed me this hysterical Australian movie, *The Castle*, and I've been thinking about it ever since. It's about a family trying to keep an airport from expanding into their backyard. The dad's obsessed with buying useless items from the *Trading Post* and the mom wears these ridiculous sweaters with puffed flowers and way too much color. When the dad tries to buy something from the classifieds in the *Trading Post* and disagrees with the price, he says, "Tell him he's dreamin!"

A terrible lawyer tries to defend the family in court, but fails miserably by misquoting parts of the Australian Constitution. The judge keeps asking the lawyer what part of the Constitution he'd like to use in his defense and all he can come up with is something like, "Well, Your Honor. It's just the vibe of the thing."

We laughed so hard and played back the best parts. It's one of the top ten funniest movies I've ever seen. It might also be funnier to watch naked.

I hadn't felt that soft, warm, cuddly vibe with someone in a long time. I love being close with a man and splitting a lazy Sunday between playing video games, eating, and mating. Missing a relationship, I acknowledged again that it was time to stop being so afraid of getting into one.

Our last night together, in the heat of passion, I told Patrick I wanted him.

"Ya have me. I'm all yours." In that moment, he was.

I grabbed on to those feelings as hard as I could because I knew they would be gone soon and so would he.

He drove me back to our hotel in the early morning hours before his shift at the car wash.

Watching him drive, I burned an image of him in my head. He parked, kissed me, and said goodbye.

"Sweet Ameerican gal. Have a wondaful rest of the time on ya great ad-venchah. Thank ya for letting me be a part of eet."

"I will. Thanks for having me." I rubbed my cheek against his and smelled him one last time, then said goodbye, crossed the street, and allowed loss to surge through me like poison. I took a deep breath, thanked the universe for the experience, and honestly let it go. Once again, I didn't die. I enjoyed myself, made a choice to spend time with Patrick, and landed the dismount.

Patrick emailed a couple of times and told me he missed me. He talked about my smile and how much he enjoyed our time together. I missed him, too, but not in a desperate way. He reminded me of what I wanted and what could be again. What *would* be again.

After Shannon and I left beautiful Queenstown, we drove all the way up to the top of the South Island. I took more pictures on that island than anywhere else on the trip. I snapped shots of deer, cemeteries, snowy mountains, rivers, and interesting street signs. The South Island is, without a doubt, one of the most gorgeous and unforgettable places I've ever seen. I'd go back in two seconds, but alas, we wanted to catch a bit of the North Island before we headed to Indonesia.

Shannon and I took a ferry between the islands. Reluctant to leave, I could already tell the North Island didn't look like its counterpart below. When we got to Wellington, it felt like we were back in a city with trams, cars, sidewalks, and people, scurrying across it all. The South Island is serene while the North Island is a lot more populated and busy.

We arrived on Halloween. Not sure how to costume Tiny Elvis, I ended up taking his clothes off altogether and shoved him in my bag for a fun night out. Sometimes, we just need to be naked.

On the street, we found ourselves surrounded by twenty-one-year-olds, prancing around in scantily clad costumes. Just like at home, people skipped by, dressed as Britney Spears and Lady Gaga. At one bar, we had to have a costume to get a free drink, so we told the bartender we were dressed as American tourists. The guy laughed and gave us a couple of shots for free.

We made headbands out of fake spider web cotton I pulled off the wall of the bar. I positioned naked Tiny Elvis on the table and made him one, too. I'm not sure why no guys talked to us that night.

After spending a few days in Wellington, we headed north. We'd been told an amazing thing to do on the North Island was to explore the Waitomo Caves. Shannon and I had read that we'd see glowworms, swim in caves, and climb up waterfalls. That was it. The brochure for the tour said something about abseiling, but I didn't know what that was.

Our cave-exploring group consisted of ten people—a mother/daughter duo, us, and some couples. Our guides set us up with wetsuits and little rubber boots. We even got helmets with lights stuck on the front. We turned on the lights and did the robot in our plastic hats. It took Shannon and I forever to get out of the dressing room because we videotaped the helmet break dance.

We tripped over our feet, hustling out of the bathroom.

"Okeee. Follow us for a leettle hike up thee heel where we'll show ya how to work the ropes," our tour guides announced.

"I hope there isn't too much climbing involved." Shannon whispered.

"I know. I'm not that strong of a climber."

We followed the group up a hill and rounded the corner to find a bunch of ropes, hanging down a small cliff.

"This is where we pricktace," the instructor yelled.

The hill was steep and ferocious. If this was practice, what were we getting ourselves into?

The instructor showed us how to harness a rope around our butts and through little metal bars clipped to our bodies. We then had to hold the rope behind our backs, hang, and creep it down, inch by inch. It was quite daunting, scaling down a hill, knowing we were preparing for a slippery cave wall.

They had woven the rope into this contraption thing, which I know has a name, but I've already forgotten it. It's crazy because we had to maneuver it with our fingers with one hand behind our backs as we went down. We were suspended in mid-air, inching down a rope that could slip out of our hands at any moment.

Following our tutorial, we trekked around the hill to a stream with a little plank going out into it. *Another fricken' plank.* We would walk the plank, harness the rope around our butts and thighs, and abseil–rappel–down through a little cave opening in the stream. It was so random. The hole opened up right in the middle of the stream.

I harnessed myself and moved down the rope. "Well, shit. I guess this is really happening," was all I could muster.

I had to creep 150 feet down into the cave. Some people were already in when my turn came up and they weren't dead, so the potential for survival existed. With sweat beads forming on my forehead, I jimmied myself along the rope slung under my butt and heard Shannon's voice from above.

"You can do this!"

All I had to do was release the rope and I would be toast. I was in charge of me. *What a concept.*

After I made it through the hole, I lowered myself along the wall of a dark cave then landed on a platform where a guy unclipped me. His name was Ja. As I hung in the dark, lost in the Kiwi accent yet again, I yelled down, "Is it Jar? Or are you saying Ja?"

"It's Ja," he replied.

I still didn't know if it was Jar or Ja, so I just called him Jim. I'm kidding. I'm pretty sure it was Ja, which was my older brother's dog's name, so I had to chuckle. I rather liked Ja. He whistled the theme song to *The X-files* as I rappelled down into the abyss.

Nice touch.

After Ja unhooked me, Shannon came down and we shivered through some pitch black caves with freezing cold water up to our ankles. We could already see glowworms on the ceiling and walls. They sparkled like stars.

Shannon was in front now and Ja clipped her to a rope, but wouldn't tell us what we were doing next. "Seet down and put ya feet up."

Reluctantly, Shannon did and without warning, Ja pushed her down a zip line. She screamed and vaporized into another cave.

Ja clipped me up next and I sailed behind her. I blew through the air and threw my head back to discover thousands of glowworms, covering the ceiling. The scene moved in slow motion. I can smell the dankness of the cave as I write this. It was just me and the worms. They twinkled, luminescent.

After the zip line, we sat on some rocks above rushing water and the guides fed us hot chocolate and sugary granola squares to give us energy so we wouldn't faint during the next stage of the journey. Our teeth chattered. The granola bar was so sugary, I couldn't finish it. So I slipped it into the outside strap of my helmet and asked Shannon if I looked like Forest Gump in Vietnam. "I do know what love is Jen-eh," I said.

Our instructor interrupted our fun. "Now ya gonna geet in these inna tubes and jump into that water there."

"That water there," rushed several feet below us under the rocky cliff. I figured it was probably a touch above freezing. I searched for a way to climb down the cliff so I wouldn't have to splash in, but no such luck. People started grabbing the tubes and jumping and we knew we needed to suck it up.

The drop put my whole head underwater, soaking my long hair. The water leaked down the back of my wetsuit like icy daggers, burning my skin. I guessed the light on my nerd helmet was waterproof because it kept shining. Then I peed my pants because I thought it would warm me up, despite the fact the guides had told us specifically not to urinate in the suits. I figured that out of ten people, someone would be doing it so why not me, too? "I mean, who isn't peeing in a wetsuit?" I whispered to Shannon.

And while we agreed it was wrong, she admitted, "I did it like an hour ago."

Unfortunately, the wetsuits were bulky and tight at our ankles so the pee had trouble escaping.

"Dude, the wizz is just sitting there."

"I know. This is gross, right? Are we gross?"

"What if it doesn't come out?"

"It has to. Just swim around and really shake your body."

The shaking didn't work so we lay down and floated through the caves with piss sloshing around our calves. The water clapped against the inner tubes... or maybe it was the pee. Our teeth chattered more.

I didn't think I'd ever been so cold. Each time I waved my arm to push through the water, frostier droplets trickled into my suit.

"Now we know youse relaxed!" The tour guy yelled down the cave. "Just a reeminda: Don't pee in the witsuit!"

"We're stone cold busted," I whispered to Shannon.

"It's not like they can smell it."

All chills and urine fears aside, the glowworms sparkled spectacularly. We found out the worms are larva and the glow comes from their shiny poo. Holding on to each other, Shannon and I drifted in our inner tubes in total darkness. My body shook, and I lost myself in the cave ceiling.

After that, the frost got all mixed up with claustrophobia when we ditched the inner tubes and walked through some new, atrociously shallow caves. I kept waiting for the hobbits to jump out and yell, "Surprise!" Some of the passageways were so small, we had to get on our bellies and wiggle around stalactites.

Next came the waterfall. Glory be to God.

Crawling, we rounded a corner on all fours to find a waterfall, shooting from above. Then, we saw the feet of the person in front of us, climbing up the fall. That person had to grasp onto little rocks and make their way up through the waterfall. Mind you, we were still underground and we were climbing into another section of cave; we could only navigate because of our headlamps. At that point, we couldn't hear each other over the booming rush of the water.

My turn came. I was shivering, both from the cold and my nerves. I'm not a rock climber, and I was terrified of slipping. Plus, the wetsuit was so heavy,

I struggled to bend my knees in it. *And if I did bend my leg, would pee spray out everywhere?* I had to climb strategically and position my feet perfectly to get up. *Push me, Dad.*

I took a deep breath and grabbed all the right rocks, making my way through like a crab spreading its limbs. I finally reached a ledge, only to be pummeled in the face by more water. I had to put my knee in the middle of the gush and grab for my life to get past it. Then, I crawled through a baby tunnel to the next passageway. I stopped for a moment to check on Shannon.

I crouched in the tunnel, trying not to allow claustrophobia to paralyze me. I forced my mind to beaches and open spaces and focused on the beer waiting for me on the other side. Finally, I saw Shannon through and we surged forward.

The guides surprised us with a video camera as we pushed through the last hole, all red-faced and freaked out. "Weeve to the camera!

"Oh come on!" Part of me wished I could go back and tell myself not to sign up for the glowworm cave tour. I also wanted that suit off my body, but I worried about the pee.

Back at the compound, they told us to take off our wetsuits and dunk them in a tank full of soapy water. The lady also said, "Meek sure if ya's peed in ya's suit, you set it aside."

Yeah, right. Like we would ever admit to peeing in our suits.

As we dunked our little booties into the water, one of the guys in the group ripped off his wetsuit and dunked it next to us. Within seconds, the air filled with the foulest smelling piss stench you could ever imagine. Everyone moaned and covered their noses. I froze and turned white. The aroma was exactly what our suits would smell like when we took them off. What were we going to do?

As everyone continued complaining and pointing fingers, we raced into the dressing room. "Just take it off fast and we'll go back out there, dunk it, and run," I told Shannon.

So, we peeled our suits off and immediately heard some of the women on the other side of the dressing room wall complaining. "What is that smell? It smills like urine in here strongly."

It really did. We rinsed our bodies and suits in a little shower as fast as we could and bolted back outside in our bathing suits. By the time we got to the suit-washing tubs, everyone else from our group was inside the lounge, drinking hot chocolate.

One member of the crew who had stayed behind, angrily scrubbed the "tainted" suit with a brush. "I kinnot believe this sheet," she mumbled.

Whistling, we sauntered over to the tank, dunked our suits twice, threw them in the pile with the others, and zipped out of there. We don't know if they found out. I like to think we got away with it. I guess peeing in wetsuits only works successfully in California.

Shannon and I stayed in New Zealand for another week. We toured half of the North Island, but I missed the South Island and my adventures (hot sex) there. I thought about snuggling with Patrick, but after a few days, his face faded and I knew I was just missing being close. We emailed a couple more times, then our connection flew out into the universe where it belonged.

C H A P T E R   1 8

Duck Nap

IN BALI, INDONESIA, motorcycles zipped by me like flies, cutting through the heat. I had to seriously watch it when I crossed the street to make sure I didn't get hit. They reminded me of riding on my father's motorcycle. His arm would become a bar around my waist and I knew he wouldn't drop me.

"Hold onto the handlebars, honey! Don't be afraid!"

Snuggled up to my dad's chest like a little bear cub, I felt protected. Flying through the air above the roar of the engine made me larger than life, just like him.

The streets in Bali were full of people, many of whom were suffering. Amidst the gorgeous beaches and architecture, trash lined the gutters and women begged with naked children standing next to them. Dinner cost a couple of bucks and I'm sure the servers made a fraction of that.

The people there were kind and wonderful, but the heat in Bali was almost unbearable, and walking in the blaring sunlight wasn't an easy task. One day, as sweat dripped down my legs, I nearly fell into an open manhole. It was so full of trash, I didn't notice the hole until my foot hovered above it.

In an effort to avoid the chaos of the city, we didn't spend a lot of time in town. We'd wake up and go straight to the beach where the waves were colossal and the surfers looked gorgeous riding them.

I surfed for the first time in Bali. We booked lessons along Kuta Beach on the southern part of the island. The surf school provided us with rash guard shirts and shorts to wear. Due to muffin-top expansion, I didn't know which size to pick on the bottoms. I attempted to pull a random pair over my hips. "Of course, these shorts are too small," I told Shannon.

"My shirt's too small. I'll go exchange them." When she returned to our dressing room with different sizes, I slipped the second pair on and couldn't get the Velcro buckle to adhere around my belly. Frustrated, I wanted to punch my fist through the wall.

"Of course, these are too tight, as well. Hi. Can I have another slice? I feel like a fat idiot."

"It's okay. I'll go get another pair." Shannon left and I stood in the dressing room, waiting in my underwear.

I turned sideways and pushed my stomach out as far as it could go. "Get in, ma belly," I whispered to the mirror as I grabbed onto the bottom of my stomach. I laughed, forcing it in and out. Then I heard the guy at the shorts bar laugh, too.

"Oh, bigga AGAIN?" he asked Shannon.

"Knock it off!" Shannon said, defending me. She returned with new shorts and handed them to me. I grabbed them and noticed they were black instead of pink.

"I don't get it…"

"Don't be mad, but you tried on the largest women's size. The men's shorts are black."

"Fuck minus." So now the guys and I would be in black shorts and the women would be in pink. My shorts would be an official announcement of my girth. I didn't even want to guess what size that meant my waist was. Trying not to show my embarrassment, I pulled the shorts on and waddled out to join the rest of the class. Relieved, I saw a woman from Germany wearing the black ones, too. I would have made a joke, but wasn't sure if she spoke English. Besides, what would I have said? "Glad to see we are both in the fat shorts club," or maybe, "Guten tag. Guess we don't need any flotation devices. This belly will do! I like pizza. Do you like pizza?"

I kept my mouth shut.

After I got over my man shorts, I posted up next to Shannon for our lesson. Our teacher was amazing. Unlike the scuba lesson, this guy went over everything thoroughly. He made us practice getting up and even told us about tides and why waves are good or bad. By the time we got in the water, I knew exactly what to do and went about it confidently.

I laughed because the waves were so weak. I wondered if they could even hold us up. I wanted to stand up on the board so badly and to my surprise, I did it on the first try. Granted, it was for about a millisecond, but by the second try, I stayed up longer. Proud as ever, my shorts and I show-ponied a bit. I put my hands on either side of my waist as a sign to the universe that we were pretty important.

That was until the instructor scolded me and told me to stop fooling around. He spread his arms out straight on either side of him. "No, no! You don't put hands like deese. Put they outta like deese!"

I nodded and straightened out on my baby wave.

I'm always at home in the water. After the first time, I had no trouble getting up. Sometimes, I cheated and bounced to my knees first, which I wasn't supposed to do. I tried not to cheat, but sometimes I couldn't help it. Even when I got tired, I worked to pop right up so I didn't get into any bad habits. Granted, the waves were wimpy and our gigantic boards were made out of thick Styrofoam, but it didn't matter. Surfing was liberating. I did have trouble with my turns the second day, but I couldn't wait to practice again.

After we surfed, we found some lounge chairs on a nearby beach and read books all day in the sun. We ogled surfers and ate pizza and all was right with the world, as long as we stayed out of our gross hotel room.

We stayed at some of the cheapest hotels of the trip in Bali. They had moldy bathrooms and the air conditioning in most rooms gave about five percent effort. Sometimes, in the middle of the night, the unit would shut off all together, leaving us panting for air in the swampy darkness. As soon as the sun came up, we'd pack a bag and head back to the beach in search of mold-free oxygen.

I finished *The Lovely Bones,* by Alice Sebold, on Seminyak Beach. It's about the journey of a murdered teenager. She follows her family around, missing them in the aftermath of her death. Observing the waves crashing near my toes, I couldn't help but wonder if my father had done the same thing after he died. *Is he following us around? Is he trying to push Dylan and me back together? Is he lonely?* I thought I felt him by me sometimes, but I couldn't be sure. I guessed I wouldn't know the answers to any of those questions until I saw him again.

Two ducks quacked in the sky above me. Duck hunting for my father had been a way of life. It was something we could do together, even though it was never my thing. I was a horrible shot and in all the times we went, I never hit one duck. I only went to hang out with him. The sun blazed bright in my eyes, so I closed them.

♋

My dad and I are sitting in a small blind, a little square pod, positioned in the water. We are decked out in camouflage and are crouched down in the pod with shotguns in our hands. Since the ducks can't see us, they fly above, creating unwilling targets.

My dad reaches into his inside jacket pocket and pulls out a flask. He takes a drink and hands it to me.

"Dad, it's 5:30 in the morning."

"But it's the nectar of the gods." He gives me a sidelong smirk.

"I'm so tired. Where are the ducks?"

"Stop talking. Be patient."

"Why are you only patient with ducks?"

Never taking his eyes off me, he swigs another drink, puts the flask back in his pocket, and doesn't answer.

I point to the shore. "Here's what's happening. I'm gonna go for a wee snooze over there. I promise I'll come back when you start shooting at all the glorious ducks that are about to come. I'm sorry, but I just can't keep my eyes open. In hindsight, I probably shouldn't have told you I'd hunt with you the morning after graduating from college."

He peers at the shore and back at me. "You're going to lie on that duck shit encrusted riverbank and actually fall asleep?"

"Yes. Watch me. I have a gift." I kiss him on the cheek, hand him my gun, and slurp my waders into the water. I have to hold my arms up and walk gingerly so the river doesn't creep over the top of my rubber pants, which stop above my waist. My father monitors my journey, so I can't falter. The water is deep, but I carefully make it to the shore without getting my body wet.

On the riverbank, I lay flat on my back with arms spread open like an eagle. My head rests on years' worth of compacted mallard droppings, but I don't care. The sun is rising and shining on my face. It feels perfect. I open one eye, lift only my head to check on my dad, and see him chuckling at me and shaking his head. Resting my head back on the earth, I fall asleep in about thirty seconds.

I never hear any shooting after that. I just wake up to my father yanking my arm and telling me to get up. He lifts me like I weigh a pound. Six ducks hang off a rope, slung across his shoulder.

"Come on, sleepy."

"That's weird. I never even heard you shooting."

∞

Ubud, Bali is a far cry from Kuta Beach. It's miles away from the water and imbedded in a jungle full of monkeys and green parrots with orange beaks. The hotel we booked could have been plucked from an exotic travel brochure. We had forty days left on the trip, so we decided to live it up and spend some money on a lavish place, for once.

Employees draped in traditional Balinese red and gold rang a shiny brass gong when we arrived. The hotel housed spiral staircases, marble walkways, two pools, and HBO. Oh, and the bathroom was like a shrine with a moon roof, a luxurious tub, and impeccable tiles. It even smelled clean.

Our first adventure in Ubud involved a colony of misbehaving monkeys. We'd read about a monkey park where monkeys come up close to you and thought it sounded fantastic. So we got a ride to the park and quickly discovered the rumors were true. Gray monkeys with little beards scurried all over the place. Babies and mamas groomed baby daddies. Some crept slowly, while others chased people who were dumb enough to buy bananas to feed them. Always afraid of contracting some form of rabies, I froze often.

"I really don't want to get some form of monkey rabies out here."

My rabies obsession can be blamed on my Aunt Lisa. I say this with a smile, because I love my aunt, but she had a major fascination with horror movies when I was little. When my dad took my older brother and me to my aunt's to spend the night, she would show us the most terrifying films. The worst one, *Rabid,* followed people who had contracted rabies and were, of course, giving it to other people in exceedingly violent ways. The scariest scene my child brain remembers was of a pale, sickly woman, bobbing and weaving on a subway train. Her eyes were all red and telltale rabies foam bubbled out of her mouth. Nobody noticed until she bit a hole in some guy's neck. Hence, rabies juice transferred.

While we watched the movie in my aunt's living room, a neighbor knocked loudly on the door to ask to borrow some eggs and scared the living shit out of all of us. Needless to say, I didn't sleep that night and the fear of rabies still lingers, all these years later.

Back at the park, we strolled down the main pathway to discover monkeys, zipping around everywhere. They walked beside us and seemed to pose for pictures. That was until I got too close to one and it hissed at me and got down in the strike position. Backing up quietly, I hoped to God it would stay put. It did.

My fear intensified as we approached a courtyard where dozens of monkeys chased tourists and screamed at each other. Taking photos, I surveyed the area to make sure no monkeys were getting ready to kill me.

In the meantime, Shannon crouched several feet away, trying to get a close-up shot of a baby monkey. Suddenly, she screeched and ran toward me with that baby monkey dangling from the bottom of her backpack. "Oh, my God! That monkey is really on there! Oh, my God!!" I screamed.

A park worker waved his arms at us. "You stop now! Monkey want to chase you and he sporting." I guessed that meant he wanted to play with her. That worker was right on, though. When Shannon stopped, the monkey let go and ran away.

"Jesus! Did he bite you? Did he scratch you?"

"No, thank God."

"What if he did and you just don't know it?"

"I'm fine."

"Let's just get out of here. I'm too scared now, anyway."

Shannon agreed and we crept out as quietly as we came in. I worried that at least one of the monkeys that lined the planter boxes on the way out would jump on me, but none did. I got all the monkey pictures I needed for life and cheered when we arrived at the front gate.

CHAPTER 19

❧

Close Your Eyes and Try

I'D BE LYING if I didn't admit how much Elizabeth Gilbert's, *Eat, Pray, Love*, inspired me to write and travel. She left her old life to find contentment abroad. Despite her struggles, she did it and her courage motivated me to be brave, too.

The book detailed her travels to visit a medicine man in Ubud, Bali, named Ketut Liyer. He read Elizabeth Gilbert's palm and told her all sorts of things about her life. Since we were in Bali, I knew we had to meet him.

I found Ketut's name on Gilbert's website and wrote it down on a piece of paper, though she also wrote that all the drivers in town would already know it. When I gave the piece of paper to a taxi driver on the street, he smiled and told us to get in. Meeting that driver was kismet, but I'll elaborate on that in a bit. He took us around a couple of dirt roads and turned left at a little sign that had Ketut's name on it. Taxis lined the gate and I figured there would be a lot more *Eat, Pray, Lovers* there, waiting to speak with the medicine man.

"Julia Robert here just two days ago," our driver beamed.

"Oh, really? Was she nice?"

"Oh, yes. She an angel." Our driver said a colorful movie crew had been shooting all over the area for weeks. It must be so gratifying for Elizabeth Gilbert to know that, not only did her journey inspire readers, but one of the most famous movie stars ever would now play her on the big screen.

We walked into the compound and saw a woman sitting with Ketut on his porch. He spoke and she listened intently. Ketut's voice sounded soft, like a little melody dancing across the courtyard. He looked old, but not his actual age of ninety-five. He held the lady's hand in his and I wondered how he had the energy to spend his days reading the palms of women seeking enlightenment. I think most of the women—myself included—simply wanted answers about love coming into their lives. *Will he sweep me off my feet? Will he love me forever?* Would I actually ask Ketut these questions?

The courtyard housed a series of small shrine-like platforms. One platform had a bed on it with all sorts of scarves hanging from the ceiling. A woman and her husband yawned in the second shrine and Shannon and I waited on a couple of couches in the third one.

Another woman waited with her young daughter nearby. She paced back and forth between the shrines while her driver worked to entertain the kid. It became clear that the two people in front of us had been waiting for a while. I didn't care. We felt fortunate to even be there.

The pathways between the shrines were ripe for people watching. Children ran by into another courtyard amidst puppies and people carrying plants and food back and forth. A light rain fell and I could see Ketut smiling as he spoke.

Our driver waited patiently on the couches with us. "How long does a reading last?" I asked him.

"Depends. Everybody different."

Ketut finished up and went over to the husband and wife waiting in the second shrine. He told them something and shook their hands. Then he came to us.

Ketut grabbed my hands in his. "Where you from?"

"California."

His eyes were blue and translucent. He had the largest smile I'd ever seen in a mouth that housed few teeth. His energy felt true. "I take break to eat and rest. I come back out later." I had no idea what later was, but I didn't mind. We were so curious about him, we made the commitment to wait.

Ketut came back out about a half an hour later. He took the pacing mom first. She burst into tears as soon as she sat down with him. I could tell she was searching hard for something and I made the assumption she longed to hear good things. He held her hand and seemed to make her feel better. She laughed like he had told her something good. Out of nowhere, the most gorgeous rooster waddled by us and I got up to follow it.

I walked through a wooden archway into a secret garden, where a fountain blew water in a halo in the center of a courtyard. A dozen people sat on various steps in front of several little cottages. It appeared Ketut's entire family lived there. Rambunctious kids ran around people working in the garden. A monkey chained up in a tree squawked. I walked over to investigate. The monkey wanted nothing more than to be fed or freed. Since I could do neither, I left a bit ashamed.

We waited there for three hours before my turn came. I sat next to Ketut on the porch and immediately sensed his discomfort by the stressed look on his face. He spoke a little, asking again where I was from then excused himself to go to the bathroom. His moaning trailed out the bathroom window. I surmised he might have a bladder infection and felt selfish for not just getting up and offering to come back later.

When he came back out, I asked him if I should leave.

"No, no. I read palm." He ran his fingers across my hand. "You will live a hundred years. You berry smart. Too smart."

He also told me I was strong and would be successful at a lot of things.

"You will marry nice boy and have two kids." *Sweet.* "You berry impatient. You need work on that."

I laughed. Smart man.

After getting up for a third time, Ketut confirmed he had a kidney infection and told me he would have to end our session. Empathizing, I felt guilty for taking his time. I thanked him for the experience and signed his guestbook. I'm not sure what I got out of the reading. It was heartwarming to meet such an interesting person, but I didn't have any epiphany moments. I already believed I would meet a nice boy and marry him; I just needed to find the courage to let a nice boy in. No one actually needed to tell me that.

We went back the next day so Shannon could get her reading. Ketut was feeling much better and he spent a lot more time with her. He told her ninety percent of the exact same things he told me, but again, we didn't care. It just felt good to be around him. Maybe I was meant to go there to be reminded that the answers are already inside of me. The experience made me think about Rumi again.

"You are the secret.

You have everything you need.

You are the medicine.

You are the cure for your own sorrow."

I am the cure. I am the remedy. It starts with me and it always had, so why couldn't I get the answers through my head and make them stick?

The next day was sensational. The rain didn't get me down and the air smelled like wet rice. It beckoned me in like the endless terraces of green, mixed with gray water along the hills of Ubud. Shannon wanted to stay in and I was delighted to take in my next Balinese experience all by myself.

I called my favorite new driver extraordinaire and he came to scoop me up for another adventure. I still can't pronounce his name, but for the sake of this writing, I will call him Balance. I say this because when I asked Balance to explain Hinduism and what Buddha has to do with it, I had no idea the explanation would last for hours, tying into the people, the elephants, and even the flowers I would embrace throughout the day.

Before I met Balance, I'd observed dozens of Balinese people, placing little square offerings in front of their houses, shops, in the streets, on tables, in their cars, everywhere. It happened every day and the offerings always consisted of a square holder made of palm leaves with grass, rice, a little Ritz cracker, flowers, and incense. The roosters eat them and so do the monkeys. I frequently had to avoid stepping on them because they peppered the sidewalks. I asked a woman about them and she said they were for God. She said they made the good come in and the bad go out. Other than that, I didn't know anything about Hinduism. I only knew that Bali was unique in that many of the places around the island were Muslim-based and the Balinese were, for the most part, Hindu.

"I don't get it. I know who Buddha is, but I don't get what he has to do with Hinduism." We were headed to an elephant park I'd been dying to see.

Balance straightened in his seat and smiled. "I explain. I study dis since I seventeen years old." As he spoke, we drove around steep hills and frail women carrying pounds of food, wood, and crafts in baskets on their heads. "We all in and out. You daughter to ya fadder and mudder. You person on television at work. You friend to odders. We all mix it together with air, with universe, with spirit. We remember not too much money and stuff. We more here than in those things." When he said the word "here," he touched his heart.

I took in his words like no other sounds existed. They were so much more than words. It was as if Balance shared the energy inside of himself with me. That energy became an extra person in the car with us.

Balance moved his hands and pointed to people on the street. "We in dis together." Sometimes, he'd stop to breathe. He told me how connected it all is—Buddha, the Hindu god of the sky, his daughter, the dog sifting through food in a pile of trash. He pointed to a little shop that displayed a window sign about meditation classes. As the sign disappeared in the rear view mirror, I saw that they offered a meditation session for twenty dollars. He explained how meditation was in his heart and a person didn't have to be at any particular place to do it. "You just have to do it, anywhere."

His words inspired me to run home and meditate, since I hadn't done it on the trip. I knew it was because I had been lazy and never felt I was in the right place. I had spent some time sitting quietly in other ways on the trip. Hopefully, that counted a little.

Listening to Balance speak and watching him steer around cows, mopeds, and people, I realized the "place" always existed. It had been inside of me the whole time. I only needed me. As the wind hit my face and green rice fields unraveled like falling cards, the words went over and over in my head.

I only needed me.

"You close eyes and just try and try. You don't stop trying. You find it in here, in ya heart." He told me there were so many things his people thought about and worshipped and prayed to, and that Buddha was just one of those things. He talked about karma and how important it was to know how behavior returns to you.

I thought about my backpack coming back to me in Portugal and suddenly wished there was something nice I could do for someone right then and there. We stopped and I bought Balance some water. When we stopped again, I bought him lunch. He answered my silly questions all day.

"What is your government like? Is the leader guy nice? Do you pray to the rice?" With mouths full of satay and curry, we chatted away. He even took me into the rice field to pull out a plant for me because I couldn't understand how the rice comes off the green stems.

According to Balance, I wasn't looking in the right place. The mature rice shoots up like wheat and the little rice guys hang on for dear life. I just couldn't see them. When I finally saw it up close, they were easy to spot; the little nub-bins hung off and waved at me.

I took a picture of Balance, holding the rice up to his face. His crooked teeth beamed through a half-moon smile. Watching him, I wanted to cry. He showed me so much that day; so much I already knew, but hadn't paid attention to because of life, because of my selfishness, and because I couldn't understand how simple it all was. The happiness and fulfillment, the letting go of pain, were as simple as Balance holding that little stalk of rice. It was all there in front of me, yet I often struggled to see it. I closed my eyes and said a prayer.

Please, God, Buddha, and the sky god, let me remember this moment and make it a part of my skin. I am the rice. I am Balance. I am the elephant that wrapped its trunk around my leg in the rain. I am my father and my mother. I am the orchids that grow out of the trees like magic. I am the rooster exploring possibilities. I am as big as everything and as small as a grain of rice.

Lying in bed that night, listening to geckos croak like frogs, I thought about my dad. I breathed him in and, miraculously, I didn't feel sad. I thought about Myles and I didn't feel sad about him, either. The thoughts went in and out with my breath like rain washing the muddy footprints we left outside our door. Deep in my bones, I let something go, for once.

I thought about Balance and of the simple lessons he shared with me. I knew what I needed and what I didn't need, and that life went on when something bad happened. The healing revolved around a journey and a process that never ends. I wanted to hold those lessons close to my heart and remind myself when I slipped.

When I feel lonely and forget that the love I have for myself is enough, when I miss my father with the same ache as the day it happened, when I check my email for a remedy that will never come, for all of these things, I have to remember I'm already there. I'm in it, I'm doing my best, and I'm okay.

CHAPTER 20

—⚘—

Because of Him

BACK WHEN I foolishly contemplated moving to another country with Myles, I got an overwhelming urge to do something drastic. About a year and a half before the trip, in the middle of writing a news story at work, I decided a psychic might be able to help me make my decision. I'd visited with a psychic once on assignment and I'm not sure why the thought popped into my head, but it did. Desperate, I needed someone to give me some direction.

I did a Google search and found a review on some obscure website of a psychic named Felix Lee Lerma. He lived nearby, so I called him. I just needed to hear from one more person that I should quit pining over Myles. I left Felix a message and he called back and said he was going out of town and could only meet on the following Wednesday. Thinking nothing of it, I took the time he had available. He said he charged $150 and I said I would pay cash, convinced that if I gave him my credit card number, he could do a background check on me. Always the skeptic, I needed him to be legit.

On the day of our appointment, Felix answered the door wearing a genuine smile and a purple shirt. He was my height with brown hair and a kind face. Books adorned the walls in his pristine apartment. Fresh air blew through the windows and I felt safe. He told me to bring a trinket that mattered and any important pictures. I brought a necklace that Myles had given me and a picture of my father sitting on the grass with my little brother. I handed them to Felix without saying a word. I didn't want to give him any more hints about my life.

I sat down on a white couch next to a palm plant. Sunlight filtered through a window onto my back. I loved that apartment and didn't feel uncomfortable at all.

Felix asked my birthday and birth time so he could do a numerology reading. Sitting in a wooden chair in front of me, he wrote something in his notebook then stopped, confused. He stared at me and sighed. He then glanced back down at his notepad and back at me. His forehead wrinkled in concern.

"What?" I asked.

Felix looked past me. "Wait," he said.

I didn't know if he was talking to the air or me. It was the strangest thing because all I could think was, what about Myles? Let's get to Myles.

When Felix spoke, it was as if someone had taken my heart out of my chest and was holding it in front of my face. "I'm sorry, Michelle. This is awkward because I'm trying to get through the numerology, but your father is here and he's incredibly impatient. He keeps saying, 'My daughter! My daughter!'"

Life paused and I crumbled into myself. Tears pulsed against my eyes. I didn't say a word and I certainly didn't let a tear fall. *This guy could still just be guessing, right?* Stoic, I didn't move.

"He's saying, 'Tell her I'm sorry. Tell her I'm sorry for the way I treated her. She's holding onto my death and I want her to let go of it.'"

Breathe, Michelle. Don't faint.

Hairs stood up on the back of my neck. The chills and silence were deafening. I might have had a stroke and not noticed. I think I said something like, "I'm freaking out."

Felix was so kind and sincere. "This is the reason you are here today. He brought you here today, specifically."

That's when it all flowed in, like a tidal wave colliding with my chest. I saw the car accident.

I'm sitting on his lap.

"Who's your favorite daddy?"

"I love you. You are the love of my life."

"Ryan, I think Dad might have died in that accident."

My little brother is jumping into my arms. My dad's broken and bloody watch is in my hand.

That was the day. October 25th. I had scheduled my appointment with Felix on the seventh anniversary of my dad's death and hadn't even noticed. I had come to Felix to hear about a man who had moved as far away from me as possible, but there was something so much more important to hear... to know.

For the next hour, I mostly cried and nodded.

Felix revealed things that no one could know, even if he had done a background check on me. He told me about a black dog running around my dad. He also said my chain-smoking grandfather—who had recently died—was with my father and Felix even waved his hand in front of his face like he could smell the smoke. He told me about the ducks on the freeway and how my dad was so into nature. Felix didn't get anything wrong. He said my dad didn't miss me because he was always around me. He said my dad frequently drove with me and he wanted me to slow down because I go too fast.

I let the tears fall and consumed every word. My familiar ache pounded like the accident had happened the day before. I asked Felix if it had hurt and if my dad was scared.

"No way. He's happy. He's here. He's in the wind and with the birds." Felix paused and laughed. "He's telling me, 'I was a hard son of a bitch.'"

My father had used the term "son of a bitch" as often as some people use words like "the" and "hi." The son-of-a-bitch thing made me a believer.

Felix explained that my father showed himself being hit as a child. He said my dad had wanted to show me the abuse to let me know he was only repeating history. It wasn't an excuse, but I believe I was supposed to understand that my father had done the best he knew how. Once I surrendered to the situation, I did believe my dad was in the room with us.

Through my sobs, I kept repeating the same thing. "But I miss him so much. I want to help him. I want him back. Where is he?"

Felix did his best to explain that my dad was everywhere. "He's in the air. He's there when you wake up in the middle of the night, confused. He's in nature." He kept telling me that my dad was sorry and that he's all right. Felix also said I'd write a book. He said my dad told him I would write our story. Writing had crossed my mind, but I hadn't started anything yet.

We talked about Myles for about five minutes. Felix said I needed to move on and I agreed.

After the experience, I moved on a bit from the Dad stuff, but not entirely. It was weird to feel close to a dead person in that way. I had started getting closure, but then it was all reopened. I'd held on to my father's death before the appointment and I continued holding on to it afterwards. Knowing my dad wanted me to move on was nice, but I still didn't know how to do it.

Before I left, Felix told me my dad said I was a fighter. "He said you do not give up and you will not take no for an answer. He said you are a fighter. You are his fighter and that will keep you moving forward."

My dad had been harder on me than anyone else. He had taught me to take care of myself and my life, no matter what.

"Don't tell me the teacher didn't tell you what the homework was," my father would say. "Go find her and ask her. Figure out what is due yourself! Don't blame anyone for things not happening for you. You go seek it out and make it happen for yourself. You are in charge of kicking ass. Nobody else, Michelle."

My father pushing me my whole life molded me into a strong, responsible adult. I don't blame other people for not doing things for me or for not making me aware of what needs to be done. I always find out first and make it happen myself. I am one of the strongest fighters I know and it's because of him. He made me this way. I spent so much time wishing he had gone easier on me, I never fully appreciated the hardcore strength he passed on to me. I focused so much on the negative, I'd forgotten much of the good.

I also totally spaced on the anniversary of his death, this year. I had worried about it coming, but then it slipped by and I didn't think about it, cry about it, or pine for it. I think I was in bed with New Zealand Patrick when the day passed, which explains why I forgot, but still, what a blessing. That date no longer controls me. My dad wouldn't want it to.

I think about the Felix experience often. I think it just means more as time moves on and I let it sink in. As past due grief filtered through me, I let Felix's words marinate more thoroughly.

"He loves you and he's sorry."

I needed to hear that then and I needed to believe it on the road. I still hurt, but that experience, and seeing it through fresh eyes, pushed me a bit closer to something. *Acceptance* is really the word I'm looking for. I needed to accept my father for who he was and I needed to believe he loved me, even when he wasn't nice.

♋

I landed my first reporting job fresh out of college at twenty-two. My father and I made the 740-mile trek from Lodi, California, to Idaho Falls, Idaho, over a day and a half. As we approached our destination, I felt nervous about him leaving me.

"Check the map again, honey. I think your street is comin' up here in a minute. How much did you rent this place for again?"

"$395 a month for two bedrooms AND a garage!"

"My God. You would never find that price in California!"

"I know, but the television station is only paying me $17,000 a year so the rent will take up most of my paycheck."

"Well, you could always get a second job."

"Doing what? Bagging groceries? I can't believe I'm a college graduate and I'm going to be living on credit cards. I hope this is the right thing to do. I hope I can become the next Diane Sawyer before I go bankrupt."

He chuckled. "You'll figure it out. You always do. What's the address?"

"675. Is this it?"

My dad pulled the truck up to the front of the house. It was pink with white trim and had a lot of grass in the front yard. "Go try it."

I hopped out and stuck the key in the lock. The door opened and made that hollow sound that echoes in an empty house. It smelled like bleach and loneliness inside. I turned around and watched my father roll the back of the U-Haul open. I didn't have a lot of furniture, so it took all of forty minutes for us to unload everything. My dad planned to continue driving six hours north to Montana to visit my grandfather, but I thought he wouldn't leave until we unpacked and ate some dinner. To my surprise, he poured some bourbon into a plastic cup to take with him and hugged me goodbye.

"Honey, I'm off."

"Already? Why?" I tried not to cry.

"Gotta beat the traffic."

"In Montana?"

"You're going to be fine. It'll give you something to do, unpacking all this, making it yours. We'll talk soon."

And just like that, he was gone. I sat on the front step, watching him drive away, wishing he loved me enough to stay.

Looking back on that day, so many years later, I see a man who probably hurt as much as I did. He didn't want to leave me there just as much as I didn't want him to go, but he didn't have a clue how to communicate that, so he left. My father didn't leave because he didn't love me; he left because he loved me a lot, at least that's the way I choose to see it now.

༼

Shannon and I spent another day with Balance before we left for the next town. We shopped and he took us out to a sacred holy water temple. The sign at the entrance said women on their periods weren't allowed in. Shannon admitted to being in her cycle and opted to stand outside.

"Just come in anyway. It's not like they're gonna check your tampon," I whispered.

"Dude, I'm not risking pissing off the Bali Gods. I'm fine out here. Go do your holy water thing."

As Balance walked me in, he pointed to people blessing themselves in water shooting from stony fountains. The water came from a pool above where hot springs bubbled around lily pads. Enormous leaves hung off the trees around us, creating a canopy.

I couldn't stand in a fountain because I didn't have the appropriate sarong to wear. Balance told me it needed to be blessed and we didn't have time for that. Instead, he told me to kneel over the side and wash my hair with the holy water. I reached as far as I could and grabbed the water to splash it over my head. It dripped down my face and I asked God to forgive me for the bad things I'd done. I also asked him to help me let go. I couldn't think of anything else, I just wanted to feel a part of *something*. As entire families bathed themselves in the water beside me, I realized I truly did.

From Ubud, Balance took us to a place called Uluwatu. Our hotel pool overlooked the ocean and we loved the view. A little chapel backed up to the pool where several weddings took place each day. It was like a wedding factory. People went in, they got it done, and then came out to take pictures. The same Shania Twain song rang out of the chapel after every ceremony, "From this Moment," and it seemed so canned, it made my stomach turn.

Shannon and I loved to watch the weddings and play the "Marry It" game.

"Why don't you marry it?" she'd ask me.

"I really like this pizza, Shannon."

"Why don't you marry it?"

"*Hells Angels* is actually a fantastically researched book."

"Marry it then."

"Why don't you marry Tiny Elvis?"

"I already did."

"I have a suggestion. Why don't you marry it and play Shania Twain at your wedding?"

"That's what they're doing right now."

I enjoyed one of our last days in Bali on a beach full of kids. I thought it would be nice to grab a lawn chair and attempt to get through some of David Foster Wallace's *Infinite Jest*, but I ended up dozing off to his heady prose. He was a brilliant writer, but his sentences stretched across entire pages and my eyes glazed over dissecting them.

I woke to kids yelping and playing amidst other people reading on lawn chairs. Hot rain trickled onto my cheeks, so I gathered my bag and hid under my umbrella, realizing how much I'd missed. The rain intensified around babies dancing with their fingertips in the air. They played the drops like upside down piano keys. Surfers tackled waves with vigor. The small storm made it more exciting. A little girl walked by me and smiled ear to ear for no particular reason. Her wet black hair stuck to her olive skin. She grinned at me as if to say she knew I was finally getting it. Now, we were both in on the secret. Life is good. Joy is happening.

I listened to Norah Jones through my headphones. "I am waiting here. Waiting for you to come home," she sang. I relished the fact that I wasn't waiting for anyone to do anything. I didn't have anything to worry about. Many of us don't, when you think about it. The downpour continued and I didn't mind. Pushing the umbrella away, I tilted my head back and let raindrops hit my face and soak my hair. "Thank you," I said to the air.

Those last days in Bali floated by. Sick of noodles, we switched back to pizza. *Shocking.* One night, we ate in a restaurant with no lights. The power went out across an entire block and people enjoyed dinner by candlelight. The kitchen cooked the pizza over a fire, so lights didn't matter. The cheesy pie tasted the same and so did the wine.

Humid days and nights disappeared before us and the next thing we knew, Balance was driving us to the airport. Once we got there, it occurred to me that we hadn't met any new people in more than three weeks. I hadn't kissed a frog or even pined over one in quite a while.

Around that time, I came to realize that having a man in my life was a lot like the frosting on an awesome cake. I love the cake fresh out of the oven. It doesn't even necessarily need any frosting. It melts in my mouth, hot and sticky. But the frosting drips down the sides, making it even more delicious. I really love that frosting, too, but I'm not empty if I don't have it. A man will become a part of the cake. He makes my life better, but he isn't the whole cake.

I am.

Trying hard to break old habits is a lot like "leaning into the sharp points," something Pema Chödrön talks about in her book, *When Things Fall Apart*. She says we need to quit running and instead, lean hard into the places that hurt. By embracing our pain, we can eventually move through it. The process isn't fun or easy, and I'm sure I'll get lonely a thousand more times, but it's worth it because taking the time to walk through, gave me the chance to finally get to know me.

CHAPTER 21

I am the Cork

WE ENDURED AN eight-hour layover in Kuala Lumpur on our way to Thailand. Shannon and I agreed to the hellacious Malaysian stop only because we saved about $500 on the plane ticket doing it that way. We arrived at the airport, got our bags, and spread out on a long bank of chairs to wait.

I tried my best to make a bed using my backpack as a pillow. My sweater served as a mask for my eyes and my blanket shielded me from the arctic breeze, shooting out of an air-conditioning vent above me. To keep them safe, I put my purse around my body and my camera close to my head. Shannon and I burrowed our other bags between us and under a bench. Our area looked like an episode of *Hoarders*, but we had no choice. Under the circumstances, I was surprised at how quickly I fell asleep.

I woke to an overhead announcement of a plane boarding for Beijing. My left eye had puffed up from sleeping on what I think was Tiny Elvis's hand, poking through my backpack. I squinted in the bathroom mirror, unsure if I looked like Quasimodo or a bee sting victim.

We got up in time to get on the plane, but through the confusion of waking up, a migraine came on with a vengeance. By the time we boarded, my eyes burned and the left one went a little blind. That's what happens when I get a migraine, which is about once a year. The plane took off and I closed my eyes long enough for a massive headache to come on. By the time we landed in Phuket, an island off the southwest coast of Thailand, I was ready to sleep in a real bed. As we approached the baggage claim, our friend, Nilima, skipped toward us. Nilima had gone to law school with Shannon and we had spent a lot of time with her in San Francisco before we'd left. She'd planned her vacation around ours so we could hang out for a whole week.

Nilima is Indian with light chocolate skin and long black hair. She's always gorgeous, but she looked especially radiant and thin.

"Nilima, did you lose weight?" I asked.

"Yeah, you are really tiny," Shannon said.

"Oh, it's walking. I just started walking to work. I still eat my pizza and burritos. I just added that thirty minutes or so of exercise every day. I lost a whole dress size."

So there it was. So simple. Walk more. My God, I needed to walk so much more. I tried not to worry about it, but staring at Nilima's svelte shoulders and pencil-thin legs made me feel even worse about my body. Acknowledging how far I'd let myself go, I tried not to compare my body to hers. If anything, she inspired me. If Nilima could do it, so could I… even though she had no weight to lose in the first place. *Don't think about it anymore, Michelle.*

When we got to our hotel, the girls wanted to hit the beach. I put some warm rags on my head to keep the throbbing down. While I didn't want to go, I didn't want to miss anything, either, so I put my suit on and tagged along.

Surin Beach was serene and cozy. The waves were a translucent light green and blue color. It was so pretty, I wanted to drink it. When I thought about it, Thailand reminded me a lot of Hawaii.

Palm trees swayed over white sand beaches and the water was so clear, we could see down to our feet. Tropical fish swam around our legs as waves brought in seashells and sea glass that stuck in the sand in colorful mosaics. Thailand is a dream on earth.

I stood on the shore, watching waves lick my toes like the tongue of a dog. I jumped in and floated out on my back, listening to the tick of the coral mixing with the flow of the Andaman Sea. Morphing into a cork, I let the sun glisten on my skin. The water bobbed me around at its whim, just as life seemed to do. While I could try to fight the current, it was so much more relaxing when I left it alone. I was getting used to being the cork. It was a lot less stressful living that way.

We spent that first night in Phuket, laughing and catching up over beers. Nilima filled us in on all of the gossip from back home. She told us who had hooked up with whom and who had gotten too drunk and made asses of themselves. The stories amused us and at times, made me feel like we were right back in San Francisco. Nilima told us nothing significant had changed and I believed her.

"You know, you guys, it's sometimes like you're still home. We email and read your Facebook posts, and it's like we're all still really in touch with you. That makes it fun. Imagine if you'd taken this trip ten years ago," she told us, sipping her beer.

She was right. It was so easy to communicate. In fact, Thanksgiving had crept up on us and we hadn't even realized it until the night before. My best friend, Jessica, and her family got on Skype so we could chat. I could almost smell the turkey through the computer screen.

Jessica's father, who'd been there for me through the years, told me he wanted me to come home so he could give me a big hug. Then he got choked up. Jessica put her arm around him and he said, "I just miss that girl."

Tears streamed down my face and I felt loved. It was so great to be able to see and hear everyone at the same time.

That night, my little sister and mother got on Skype, too, and Erika recited her third grade pigmy rabbit report to Shannon and me. We listened in and tried not to giggle. No one is as cute as my little sister. She's a constant source of entertainment.

"The pigmy rabbit is timid, which means shy. The pigmy rabbit has lots of babies. The piggy rabbit..." God she's funny. So yes, technology helped in easing the homesickness. With only nineteen days left on the trip, I couldn't wait to put my arms around my mother and sister for real.

Michelle Elaine Kennedy

After the three of us filled our bellies with copious amounts of Thailand's Tiger Beer, we ran through the rain back to our hotel room. The water pounded hot from dark clouds above. For a second, I stood with my hands up to the sky and thought about that awesome crescendo near the end of *The Shawshank Redemption* (best movie in life), where he swam through shit to get to the other side to escape. I was suddenly Andy Dufresne, with arms outstretched to the rain clouds. I smiled then laughed at my ridiculousness.

Thunder crashed and I thought of Jack Kerouac in the mountains at the end of *Dharma Bums*. He has a moment where it hits him and he says, "Oh. I'm happy." Just like that. The rain hit my face and I felt happy, too. With dirty hair, bigger hips, and chipped off toenail polish, I felt just fine.

My Aquarian soul burned so bright that night, I decided we should swim in the pool and feel the raindrops on our faces a little more. I put on my bathing suit, cannonballed in like a child, and floated around until the girls got in with me. We bobbed on our backs, still and free, so all our ears could hear were raindrops pounding the water like mini torpedoes. Grabbing Shannon's hand underwater, I thanked her through my heart for sticking it out with me on the trip. She thanked me back and we segued into the handstand competition.

I didn't dream about my father that night. Instead, I morphed back into a news reporter.

I'm struggling to write my script and make my live shot while trying to put on make-up at the same time. I'm fidgeting with my hair and thinking about the best direction to stand so the wind won't blow my bangs in my face during my report.

The producer calls, frantic. "Why haven't you turned in your package yet? You are on in ten minutes!" I'm so tense. My shoulders ache and my head throbs. Are my facts straight? Will they fire me? Will I look pretty enough on camera? Will I sound smart enough? I slam the phone down and realize I'm not supposed to be there. "Wait, I'm not a reporter anymore."

I wake up and sit up in the dark, stunned I lived that life for almost eleven years. Why I didn't suffer a thirty-something-year-old heart attack is beyond me. When my breathing calmed, I heard the wind rustling through the palm trees outside.

I never have to do that again.

182

Nilima, Shannon, and I spent the next several days cruising around to various islands. We spent some time at a luxurious Sheraton in a place called Krabi. I booked the room using points I had garnered from over-spending on my credit card. It was funny how that worked. I felt good about getting a sweet deal on a room, but guilty for spending money on my credit card to get there. Credit card payment woes aside, the hotel was amazing. Several pools stretched across the property. The clearest water kissed the white shore nearby as a row of palm trees curled around it like a crescent moon. We swam, read in hammocks, and slept in the sun. Although the skies were clear as glass, a bit of a cloud formed above me during that time. I thought about the trip ending and felt nervous about moving from fantasyland back to reality. Going back worried me, but seeing my family again warmed my heart, so I tried to hold onto that.

Every night, we watched a family band from the Philippines play popular cover music in the hotel bar. An aunt and her niece sang while the aunt's husband played piano. Some songs came out better than others, but as the days went on, we looked forward to seeing the band. High season hadn't hit yet and sometimes, we were the only audience members clapping as loud as we could with each rendition of Tina Turner's, "Simply the Best." They pronounced it "Simply Da Best," which we loved.

Our last night at the Sheraton, the band performed on an outside stage that had been set up by the beach. The moonlit stage looked dreamy and that Shakira song had never sounded better. Only about four other people sat at tables around us as we sipped cocktails and tried to guess each song before the band sang the words. I thought about how much I loved to sing. I had grown up singing in various choirs and plays. Before the trip, I had sung with the Glide choir in San Francisco. It's the same choir that was featured in Will Smith's movie, *The Pursuit of Happyness*, and the experience was incredible. I wasn't great, but I could carry a tune. Suddenly, I got the urge to showcase my skills.

"Do you think they would let me sing?" I asked my friends.

Nilima and Shannon giggled with excitement and encouraged me to ask.

"Can you ask them if I can sing later?" I asked the waitress.

"Yes, I ask dem." As she walked away, nervousness flooded in like it always does. I knew I couldn't back down when I saw the niece approach our table.

"My name Guy. What you want to sing?"

Okay. Breathe. This is happening. "How about Joss Stone? Right to be Wrong?" The liberating ballad is about going out on your own and becoming a strong, independent woman. *How fitting.*

"Yes, we got dat song. You be first after we break."

I pounded a beer. When I got to the stage, my hands started to shake. Trembling, I turned around to find only two other people sitting in the audience next to Nilima and Shannon. I had nothing to worry about except worry itself, but it wouldn't go away.

Just do it, Michelle.

"I've got a right to be wrong. My mistakes will make me strong." Okay. I got through the first words and didn't die.

After that, I softened my shoulders and sang my heart out as Shannon and Nilima whooped and hollered from our table. I enjoyed the experience, once I realized I was safe. The reality is, most of the time I am safe. Sometimes I just forget.

I watched Shannon zip around like a parent, taking pictures from every angle. It made me feel good to see how much she cared. When I got back to the table, my party of two clapped and cheered as loudly as they could.

"Gosh, I felt like my kid was on stage for the first time or something. Man, that was awesome. Another round of drinks!" Shannon yelled.

She was so happy for me, this person I hadn't even known two years before. We had embarked on the trip and made it great together, anyway. I felt thankful for her friendship, listening to her recap the last few minutes with Nilima.

I believe it was all meant to be: the song, the trip taken with that exact person, my life, the ups and downs. It's all always meant to be, even when we can't see it at the time. I needed to remember that on the in-betweens when anxiety peaked. *Just breathe until another moment like this comes. It will all make sense, eventually.*

As the band wound down, Shannon requested they sing Heart's "Alone." The three of us had seen Heart in concert a year before and we absolutely loved that song. The aunt said she would do it, but only if I came and sang it with them. I jumped at the chance because I wasn't nervous anymore. The aunt took care of the first part, while I waited patiently for the chorus. A couple more notes and we made it.

"'Til now, I always got by on my ownnnnnn. I never really cared until I met you." I belted the words out, hoping Heart would hear me back in Los Angeles. I even surprised myself. I actually kind of wailed. "And now it chills me to the bone. How do I get you aloooone?" Don't get me wrong; I cracked on some of the high notes and came in too early on one of the lines, but overall, it might have been my greatest karaoke performance yet.

Nilima and Shannon screamed below the stage. Each time they cheered, I sang harder. What a triumph. By then, we were the only people left. My audience of two was the best I could have ever asked for. I might have startled my fellow stage mates a bit, but I will never forget that night.

After we left Krabi, we took off for the island of Ko Lanta, where we spent more days on the beach and in the water, snorkeling. Then, we cruised in a long wooden boat to another island, Koh Phi Phi Leh. People told us it was special, but we had no idea how right they were.

CHAPTER 22

Jumping Through Fire

THE TSUNAMI OF 2004 destroyed most of Thailand's Koh Phi Phi Leh. The tiny S-shaped island is so thin, we could stand on one side of it and see all the way to the other side where the water started again. The tsunami wave destroyed most of the few resorts on the island and killed more than 1,000 people. When we arrived five years later, the island looked immaculate, like nothing bad had ever happened there.

Our taxi boat couldn't motor all the way to the shore because the water was too shallow at the pristine and minuscule beach. Not knowing what to do with our bags, Shannon, Nilima, and I looked around for a little life raft. Our boat driver finally pointed to two men who appeared to be hotel employees, wading through the water toward us.

"Oh. Are they coming to grab our bags?" Shannon asked.

Our driver nodded.

Sure enough, two superheroes loaded our luggage on their backs and waded in water past their thighs to the shore.

We followed, doing our best to hold our skirts and purses above the water.

Standing on the shore drying off, I wondered how water could look so light green and blue at the same time. Palm trees swayed like silk sheets in the wind and next to Whitsunday Island in Australia, Koh Phi Phi Leh was, without a doubt, the most stunningly beautiful beach we'd visited so far.

I met Jasper and his three Canadian friends in the lobby of our hotel while we were in the process of booking a snorkeling trip. Jasper asked us to join his group because the boat was cheaper for everyone if we booked the trip together. The group seemed nice, so Nilima, Shannon and I said yes.

Jasper towered above Chris, Sean, and Barry, with a full head of brown hair, blue eyes, and a crooked charismatic smile. His friends must have had a tough time hooking up with Jasper around. Sparkly and sweet, he was hands down, the Alpha of the group.

We took off with them at eight the next morning and headed to the beach where they filmed the movie, *The Beach*. Our boat was skinny and wooden, like the ones in movies, with colorful scarves tied to the bow. We chatted it up while everyone took pictures of the water and the cracked, oval-shaped rocks shooting up from it. Something about the way the rain broke down the rocks made them appear to teeter over toward the ocean. It was a sight to see, especially since the crystal blue water was so beautiful around the harsh rocks.

We swam, snorkeled, and took silly pictures of each other. The beach from *The Beach* was worth the trip. It really did look like some special, secluded sanctuary, complete with palm trees, clear water, and about 500 tourists.

Jasper and I talked a lot on the ride home, but his friend, Sean, kept interrupting, so I couldn't get a read on the situation.

"I'm in law school. Almost done. This is my celebration vacation," Jasper told me.

"How is that possible? You seem so young."

"We get it done faster in Canada." He was adorable, exceptionally tall, and smart.

Jasper and Sean did Rob Burgundy impressions when I told them I used to be a news reporter.

"The human torch was denied a bank loan," they said, imitating Will Ferrell. They were pretty cute.

Then Jasper and I moved on to more serious topics.

"What will you do when you get back?" he asked.

Let's see. I will pull my head out of my ass, stop hooking up with dudes at bars, make peace with my father's death, and grow up. "I'll finish my Master's at San Francisco State and teach college students how to be reporters." That was true, too.

After more swimming and jumps off our boat, the guys invited us on another boat, that would take us to a different part of the island, for beers later that evening. The three of us thought it sounded fun, so we said yes.

When I found myself taking a little more time with my hair that night, I realized I was a bit more attracted to Jasper than I'd originally thought.

Jasper smiled at me when we got in the second boat. He looked gorgeous, but he had gelled his hair so I had to give him shit.

"I mean, who's using styling gel in Thailand?" I joked. He was more made up than me. *No surprise there.* It reminded me of the days when I'd get ready and wash my hair on a regular basis. Would I go back to that when I got home or settle into a hybrid routine of cleanliness, primping, and sometimes not primping at all? I did wash my hair that night and felt pretty in my black cotton sundress that I'd worn about thirty-eight times.

We got off the boat to find musicians, hundreds of people, and fire dancers on the beach. As we walked closer, we saw a group of performers spinning burning batons. I couldn't understand how they didn't accidentally catch themselves on fire.

The seven of us found a restaurant, ate pizza, and entertained each other. Jasper and his friends performed some magic tricks with coins and we screamed like kids at a birthday party. Nearby, a crowd of people gathered around the fire dancers. Two men had begun swinging a long, burning jump rope between them. People lined up and took turns jumping in as the rope crackled around them. It took the shape of a fiery sideways tornado.

Jasper darted off to check it out.

We paid our bill, followed him, and approached the flaming spectacle. Music filled the air as people jumped, terrified. Sometimes they'd mess up and step on the giant rope, but it never seemed to burn their skin. It had something to do with the kerosene the guys doused the rope with. Something about that chemical made the flames stick to the rope and not to the people jumping. One guy stepped on the rope with bare feet, but it didn't burn him. He just ran around and got right back in again.

Ecstatic, our guys took the plunge and jumped into the fiery circle. We snapped pictures, fascinated by the shapes and forms. After a few minutes, I knew I needed to get in, too. As always, if I didn't try, I knew I'd regret it. Chris and Barry helped me time the jump, while Jasper waited for me on the inside. I breathed easier knowing he'd be in there with me.

"One, two... Go!"

They pushed me in. Exhilaration carried me in with Jasper. Sensing my trepidation, the rope swingers slowed their rhythm so I wouldn't mess up. Jasper jumped in front of me and the world slowed as we synchronized.

Music blared and burning kerosene created a circle around our bodies. I watched him; he watched me. My friends screamed and cheered us on. My hair loosened out of my ponytail as heat waves danced around my bare toes. Everything blurred except for Jasper's face. I was in one of those crazy, exuberant moments I loved.

When I jumped out, the rope smacked my bare thigh, but it really didn't sting. The flames simply left a black mark that I brushed away. Jasper and I were so revved up, we took each other's hands and ran off to join a dance party nearby.

We danced for hours with our friends and hundreds of other people. Hair flew and stuck to sweaty faces. Bare feet pounded the ground. The music boomed. Somewhere in the frenzy of it all, Jasper pulled me close and kissed me. He held my face and took me in. Just us. Quiet. We were in the bubble. I love that fricken' bubble. And boy, could that one kiss. Those hours between dancing, laughing, and face-sucking were some of the best of the trip. I almost jumped out of my skin.

We didn't load back into the boat until five o'clock in the morning. When we added it up, the seven of us had danced and partied on that beach for ten hours. It seemed like only a couple because the time just buzzed by.

After the boat ride back, Jasper and I headed to his room. He made his friends sleep on lawn chairs out by the pool so we could have some privacy. I wish I could say I remember everything we talked about in his bed, but I can't. We danced for so long and were so tired, I struggled not to fall asleep in mid-sentence. He did tell me how confused he felt about school and what to do next.

"There's just so much bullshit involved in the legal field. I don't even know if I want to be a lawyer anymore." Jasper played with my hair and kissed me. *Stay awake, Michelle.*

Through our haze, we fooled around, but fell asleep in the process. I guess life is like that. We get so excited to arrive somewhere, then sometimes fall asleep when we get there. It didn't matter, though. I enjoyed every hazy minute.

"I can't believe I only just met you. I wish I had more time," Jasper told me, packing his suitcase the next morning.

Story of my life.

Still curled up in the sheets, I sighed. Timing, really is everything. One person was always either getting out of a relationship or moving away. Someone was always too young or too old, or they were about to leave on a plane to go back to their home country.

Jasper kissed me goodbye and told me to sleep as long as I wanted. Watching him go, I felt acceptance, again. No matter what came my way, I could handle it. I didn't feel anxious. Instead, I felt content and dozed off again.

♂♭

I'm standing in a room at a factory. I can see someone coming around the corner. My heart pounds. The anticipation is killing me; Myles is coming. Deep breaths. He rounds the corner.

He looks exactly the same. His eyes are as bright as ever. His facial hair is all cute around his mouth and his smile gets me good. I can't wait to spend time with him.

I'm surprised, though, as he stands in front of me because suddenly, I don't know what I want. I was so thrilled and now he's here, and I'm not feeling what I thought I would. He leans in. I can smell him. He smells the same—like soap—and I melt a little. I pull back to absorb him. We start catching up.

"I read your book, Michelle. You know, there are a lot of grammatical errors in there. You're using the wrong verb tenses and there are misspellings."

I smile as the words come out. A fifty-pound weight lifts off my shoulders. I see the fights in my head. I cried so many nights over him. Then, I remember; this is Myles. His need to be right supersedes everything else. He spent so much time correcting me and arguing over the stupidest things, it became our relationship. I was miserable.

"I don't want you anymore. I'm sure of it now." And that was that. I had my answer.

Myles suddenly turns old and as he walks away, his hair falls out, leaving a trail behind him. I'm not sure what that symbolizes, but I'm glad I don't chase after him. I watch him walk away and I finally let him go.

⸙

I've heard the theory that women pick partners who resemble their fathers. The model says that women subconsciously pick someone like their dad—in my case, someone who is hard on me—then they try to change him. If we can change the boyfriend to make him be nice, it will somehow heal the wounds of our childhood. Apparently, even though people try this, it never works because we can't change people. We also can't expect someone to heal wounds they didn't create. I had to heal my childhood pains myself.

Myles and my father were similar in that they could be sweet and charming one minute and then incredibly cruel and biting the next. Both held me with big strong arms then, occasionally, crushed my spirit with big strong words. They could both be emotionally unavailable and both had trouble putting me first. They also made my heart drop when they walked into the room because I loved them so much. They were two of the most charismatic and interesting men I've ever known. I wanted my kindness to melt their hearts and make them love me more, but it didn't.

When I look back though, I don't feel angry. I believe they gave me the best they had at the time, and honestly, that's all I could ask for. I know they loved me in their own way. Forgiving them sets me free to love myself in all the ways they could not.

CHAPTER 23

That's My Girl

EXPLORING THE STREETS of Bangkok at night was like trying to survive inside a pinball machine. Lights flashed as people yelled in our ears. Rickshaws and homemade carts pulled by men on motorcycles blazed by and it felt like the streets were moving. In the lanes of Bangkok, I was a ball, bobbing and weaving to stay in the game. If I didn't pay attention, I might get sucked down some dark alleyway, never to be seen again.

When we got to Bangkok, we were relieved to find Nilima had booked us a room at an exquisite hotel, The Shangri-La. I finally knew first-hand what the saying meant.

Our room revealed a panoramic view of the city. Baskets welcomed us in the bathroom full of fancy shampoo and huge bars of soap. The three of us took long showers and put on billowy robes so we could sit and watch the end of *Twilight* on HBO for the tenth time. Once we relaxed, we got all dolled up and took to the streets to find a popular restaurant called Larb, something we'd all read about.

Shannon, Nilima, and I had eaten a combination of Pad Thai and green curry for the past week. Never sick of it, I knew we'd order the same thing again.

A pimped out tuk tuk shuttled us to our destination. The tiny motorized rickshaw with open sides had silver rims and painted seats. Lights shot across the roof like fireworks. It was manned by a slightly crazy driver. He wiggled his fists on the steering wheel and made the thing jerk from side to side. We screamed as he blazed forward, faster and faster. I held on, trying to forget about safety.

"You like it? Dis Bangkok!" our driver screamed over the engine.

What a change from Koh Phi Phi Leh. Exhaust plumed from the cars, zipping around our miniature machine. I wondered how long we'd last. Jerk right. Jerk left. I already missed the quiet.

After a delectable dinner of Pad Thai and green curry, we found a massive night market and stopped to shop. The market took up an entire fairground. Booths and stalls twisted and turned across the property. Merchants sold everything from clothes, food, shoes, birds, watches, massages, dragon eggs, magnets; you name it.

We explored for an hour. I bought a necklace for my cousin, Nicole, and stopped, exhausted. I told Shannon and Nilima I wanted a foot massage and would meet them later. Just like in Bali, there were massage places everywhere in Bangkok. I wanted a half-hour massage, but the guy at the massage parlor I approached wasn't having it. He insisted on an hour and wouldn't budge on the price. I bent around him, looking at the dozens of people getting their feet rubbed inside. I just couldn't understand what the big deal was.

"You just take an hour and cut it in half. That's a half-hour."

"No half-hour. An hour better!"

"Dude, I want a half-hour. How much? Why? Why can't you just do it?"

"Okay. 200 Baht."

An hour was 250 baht. "No way. That's almost what an hour costs. I can only stay for a half-hour." He stood there, shaking his head. I couldn't figure out why he wouldn't want to take some money instead of none, but he let me walk away. I landed on a bench and pouted, wishing I had just said yes. I wanted a foot rub, but then again, it was the principle of the thing. All I could think about were the people back in Bali.

From my experience, Balinese and Thai people are different. In Bali, retailers often don't tell you a price. Storeowners just ask what you feel like paying and take it. I think I ended up paying more and bargaining less with the Balinese because they were so chill. Thai merchants are tougher and aren't afraid to grab your arm and literally pull you into a shop to get you to buy something. As I pondered these differences, a rat ran into a bush by my feet.

Gangly and black, the rat scavenged through a pile of trash. Wow. I don't think I've ever found a better place to put the word "scavenged" until now. He truly scavenged. He worked right by my toes, but I didn't worry.

"Hey, rat. You know where I can get a good price on a half-hour foot massage?"

"Hey, Michelle. He was only asking six dollars. When did you get so cheap?"

Duly noted.

The massage was only equivalent to six American dollars. Why didn't I just pay him and get it? My ego needed to win, that's why.

Haven't I learned anything?

I stayed with my rat for what seemed like an hour, not even considering rabies. I scrutinized the people getting their feet rubbed through the window and felt lame. I should have just bought the foot rub.

Get over it.

I thought about Jasper, then wondered what the man of my dreams was doing at that moment. I wondered what he looked like. I missed him and didn't know him at the same time.

In my dream that night, I was back at my family's favorite camping spot in the Sierra Nevada.

⌘

Dad is pulling me by the hand up mini cliffs along a bustling stream full of trout. I'm faltering to keep hold of my fishing pole and his hand at the same time.

Don't fall, Michelle.

"Okay, sweetie. Now, listen. If Daddy falls in and gets hurt, you follow this river back the way we came. Does that make sense to you?"

"Yeah, Dad."

"I'm serious. It's really important."

"Yes, Dad. I hear you. I understand."

"That's my girl."

We fish all day, just he and I. The sun blazes on crystal clear water as we hook trout after trout. I try to sing and talk, but he shuts me down.

"Hey, Chatty Kathy. You'll scare the fish away."

"Oh, sorry. I can't help it."

He smiles. I know he loves me in spite of my jabber mouth. I grab his arm and touch his gold watch. I try to forget I'm dreaming. The watch is whole and unbroken, like him. I know he's gone, but for that moment, I hold on until the sun comes up.

୨୧

A few days before we left to go home, I went out on my last walkabout by myself. Shannon wanted to sleep in and I welcomed the opportunity to spread my wings and float around solo. Each time I did, I felt stronger, braver, and more independent.

I skipped off the steps of our hotel and into a cab. "The Grand Palace, please!"

"You want to see temple?" the driver asked.

The language barrier stacked up like a pile of concrete blocks. Thailand proved to be the toughest language clash of the trip. All of the countries we traveled to spoke some English, but much of Thailand did not. I didn't expect special treatment; I was just spoiled by my other experiences.

"No. That huge palace. The big one. The Grand Palace."

"You want floating market?"

Help me.

He finally got me a block from the palace.

"Stop here!"

Close enough, I guess.

The Grand Palace property is made up of dozens of buildings, adorned with gold. They are radiant, even from far away. As soon as my feet hit the ground, a pushy guy told me to go to a specific gate nearby. Exhausted and not thinking clearly, I obeyed until what I thought was a palace employee cornered me.

"Da Palace close 'til three o'clock for prayer."

"Then it opens back up? I thought it closed at 3:30?"

"No, you come back at three. First you get in tuk tuk tour of city!" He pointed to a guy who seemed to be waiting for me on the curb.

"No way, man. I'm gonna go kill a sandwich across the street. Then I'll come back. Thanks."

At the sandwich shop, I downed a bag of barbeque chips and told a gal from New York what had happened.

She immediately set me straight. "Haven't you read the books? That's a scam to get you to take the tour in the tuk tuk. The palace is wide open. See?" She pointed to an open gate I hadn't seen.

I felt stupid. Inside the palace walls, hundreds of people walked around, admiring the property. "Dang it! Thanks so much."

After I ate my turkey and cheese, I moseyed back over. The palace was magical. Gold buildings stacked onto other gold buildings of various shapes and sizes. Gold flakes and gold squares covered statues of weird animals and little Buddhas. Paintings hopscotched around towering walls that led to endless walkways and new courtyards to be explored.

When I couldn't handle any more gold statues, I made my way out to a dock and climbed aboard a boat with thirty other people. It was like a public bus on water. The boat-bus took off and I went along for the ride, deciding not to worry where I was going, for once.

The rumbling motor filled the air around us. Fish splashed next to houses on the water. I studied abandoned buildings and watched kids jump off a dock. A baby slept on his mom's shoulder in front of me as the wind blew flecks of river in my face. Twisted weeds floated by. We cruised under bridges and in front of a huge abandoned building that was partially burned. The boat approached another dock and I figured I should formulate my next move.

When I stepped off the boat, I had no idea where I'd landed. I felt exhilarated; this was a neighborhood I hadn't read anything about. It would be my secret. I saw shopping stalls and a food market in the distance. The spicy aromas drew me in, so I followed.

The market I stumbled upon appeared endless, like a Thai mirage that stretched for miles. I heard people chopping things on cutting boards next to duck and other fried foods, sizzling in grease. I walked past eels in buckets and duck heads hanging from strings. Rainbow colors of curry dishes spread out like fans as an old woman sat behind them, anticipating a sale. I marveled, wide-eyed, over fried crickets and frog legs packed in plastic white buckets. The frog legs reminded me of gigging frogs at age nine with my father and older brother.

"Goddammit, you guys! Git heem!" my dad yips.

We have just finished a frog-gigging excursion in a slough near the house and my father is cutting the legs off the live frogs we speared. Ryan and I are in charge of catching the frogs that slip out of my dad's hands and onto the floor of our barn.

"Daddy, he's running too fast," I squeal, dipping underneath the four-wheeler parked by the door. "I think he's under here."

My dad flicks his gut-covered fingers in the air. "Well how is it possible he got that far? He only has one leg left."

"Dad, you only got half of it. He has a leg and a stump. He's movin' fast."

My brother now has his head under the four-wheeler, too.

The frog hops sideways between us.

I catch the frog and lose it in the same second. "Ahhh! He's slimy!"

My brother laughs.

My dad cuts more legs off and laughs, too.

Ryan and I chase the fugitive under the trailer and continue the hunt.

Deeper into the market, a dad and daughter sat glued to a television broadcasting a Thai boxing match. I snapped shots of crickets, the dad holding the daughter in his lap, and pans of fish guts. Some of the pictures creeped me out, but most captivated me. I captured a bucket of frog intestines; the picture is disgusting and awesome at the same time. Fat outlined the red and blue frog insides like a ribbon of white.

Confidence walked with me on that stroll through that market. I heard people singing and laughing and felt safe, even though I wasn't sure if I was even in Bangkok anymore. I rode on that boat for an hour and couldn't imagine how I was going to communicate with a cab driver how to get back to the hotel. It didn't matter, though. I was content with guts, fried bugs, and a day spent with interesting strangers.

When I did find a cab driver, he couldn't understand my directions and drove away. Concern crept in until another driver approached and spoke some English. It took my savior an hour and twenty minutes to get me back to the hotel. The ride cost only eight dollars. *Unbelievable.*

I guess I had been pretty far out there. *Whoops.*

Shannon and I said goodbye to Nilima and took a small plane back to the beach on the western coast of Phuket. We didn't do much of anything, those last days. In a way, it felt like the trip had already ended, almost like we were just going through the motions.

Canadian Jasper wrote when he got back home. *We met lots of interesting people, but I must say, you were by far the most fun, nicest one I had the best time with. You're a good egg.* He was a sweetheart and a great last guy to end the trip on.

As Shannon and I enjoyed our final sunset, we recapped favorite places and people.

"My mom, she make deez plum cakes for you," Shannon said.

"Ohhh the food in Tuscany. I'll never be the same again."

"Dude. We jumped off a bridge!"

"Ireland! I wish we'd spent more time there. Man, that place was pretty."

"Remember *The Lord of the Rings* kayaking instructor? Funyak!"

"Don't pee in the witsuit!"

Once it got dark, a guy walked by, selling wish balloons. They were made of a white paper bubble, and we were supposed to light a fire under them. We were instructed to make a wish, then let them fly out over the sea. The man lit the balloons for us. I grabbed the sides of mine and let it go. Closing my eyes, I imagined the loss of my dad and everything else that hurt, floating above the water with the balloon. *Blow away, pain. Keep blowing away.*

I wished I would keep trying and learning when I got home. I also wished to meet a man with whom to share my life. I wished for him to overlook my scars and love the old me, the current me, and the me to come. I hoped he would understand how hard I tried to get to him in one piece.

As we lay on our lawn chairs, watching the balloons shrink into a purple sky, tears blurred my vision. I cried because I already missed Shannon. She planned to move to Chicago when we got back. Happy for her, I tried not to think of it as another loss.

Shannon had made the trip fun for me. She made me laugh, supported me, and stuck it out through the annoying and hard times. The trip, my process, everything that happened, involved her and for that, I felt grateful.

Cultivating my relationship with Shannon taught me a lot about love. I hadn't expected it to, but through my interactions with her, I learned that love is about accepting someone for everything they are and staying instead of running when times got tough. Love means thinking about that other person and trying to make their day nice by listening, or even giving them some Mentos when they're sick. Love is about reaching beyond my own needs and pushing selfishness aside.

Before the trip, I'd spent so much time looking for love, I'd never understood how to find it within. The journey forced me to sit quietly with Michelle on lawn chairs, planes, planks, long-tail boats, and countless beaches. The stillness of doing a whole lot of nothing taught me that I am not so bad to hang out with, and there's a lot of love in my heart. Just because you are by yourself doesn't mean loneliness has to sink you. If you believe in God, the universe, or simply something bigger than you, taking care of you, you are never truly alone when you think about it. Traveling taught me that *I* am actually the love of my life.

I let my father go a little more each day, but he will never truly be gone. The way he died and the circumstances surrounding his death still come up in my dreams, but the dreams are changing. Lately, we fish a lot more than we say goodbye.

I finally realized the roadblock that kept me from grieving my father's death was me. I hadn't been able to move forward because I blamed my dad for the things he'd done and hadn't done. Traveling allowed me the time and space to slough and peel my resentments off, like the old skin of a snake. I used to think that hardened skin protected me. Now, I see that the weight of it kept my feet frozen in the bitter sludge of animosity. By making peace with our relationship, I opened my heart to create a new image of my dad in my head.

When I think of my father now, I see a man who gave me life, love, strength, a college education, and an ambition not everyone possesses. I'm not a quitter and I don't hide from the things that scare me. Maybe it takes me some time to stop being anxious, or sad, but I never abandon trying, and that's because of my father. When I miss my dad now, I smile with gratitude.

I've found there is no quick fix for getting through painful losses and situations. I think for me, courageously facing my grief and letting the tears fall when they needed to changed everything. Sifting through the thorny spots while playing with the occasional penis in foreign countries helped, or maybe just distracted me, but it was all part of the process. Allowing the pain to cut into me made the biggest difference. I confronted my monsters and over time, I know I will continue to recover.

I'm not a healed woman; I don't think anyone is ever fully healed. I *am* someone who falls into reality like it's a fluffy bed. My hair spreads out when my back hits and I now breathe a sigh of relief. I stare at the ceiling like I stare at the sky. What's next and how will I handle it differently? What can I let go of today? How can I give? How can I accept myself and those around me with more compassion? Most importantly, how can I bring it back and remember the truth? Rumi always reminds me:

> *Don't go off sightseeing.*
> *The real journey is right here.*
> *The great excursion starts*
> *From exactly where you are.*
> *You are the world.*
> *You have everything you need.*
> *You are the secret.*
> *You are the wide opened.*

Don't Pee in the Wetsuit

Don't look for the remedy for your troubles outside yourself.
You are the medicine.
You are the cure for your own sorrow.

The remedy had been inside of me the whole time. It took circling the globe to find that simple answer. It's silly when I think about it.

The moon lit Tiny Elvis's face on the nightstand that last night and I thought about lying in my own bed back home in just another day. I couldn't believe the six months that changed my life had now come to an end. Michelle, the courageous person I finally took the time to know, nodded off in peace.

ℭ

I'm sitting at the end of a wooden dock with my father. Our bare feet dangle in the water. He's baiting my hook with a worm I don't want to touch.

"How are you, Dad? Really?"

"I'm so good, honey. You have to believe me when I say that." He wipes worm guts and dirt on the thigh of his Levis.

"I want you to be good back on earth."

"I'm there. You know I'm there."

I grab onto his arm and see sunlight sparkle on the watch.

He casts the line and it hits the water. "Michelle, you are okay, too. Do you see that?"

I look back up at my dad's beautiful, unshaven face. "I do, Dad. I promise, I do."

My father wraps his arm around me and I finally believe him.

This is my
lucky penny,
Have it

Seeing Dylan

I STOOD ON the sidewalk, watching him park the car.

His head almost touched the ceiling of the Toyota. He looked like he did at ten. He stepped out of the car and suddenly, Dylan wasn't ten. His six-foot frame walked toward me and I lost it. He moved quickly, swallowing me with his arms.

I fell apart and Dylan held on tight.

Totally present, he took care of me. My baby brother met me halfway so we could start over.

I didn't know exactly what we were starting, but at least it was something. I wasn't dreaming anymore. I felt happiness through my tears. *Finally.*

Epilogue

I WROTE THIS book as a way to grieve, and now I find it connects me with others going through the same feelings.

I started on the first draft more than six years ago. Reading it today, I hear a different woman's voice. I wish I could go back and put my arms around her—my younger self—and suggest she quit beating herself up. I am compassionate to how much fear ruled my thinking. I am also grateful to see the transformation I've made since then. Writing this kicked off a path to forgiveness that absolutely changed the way I see others and myself. Today, I embrace the younger version of myself and remind her that she is loved and she did the best she could. She made it through to the other side of grief and self-doubt.

Grief is incredibly tricky. It was so frustrating, knowing so many years had passed and I still felt sad. I have learned, though, that there is nothing wrong with me. Grief takes as long as it takes. For me, finally facing the grief allowed me to walk across the scalding hot coals I had dreaded for years. I am so glad I took the time to do this, and surprisingly, there are no scars on my feet.

When I came back from traveling, I did see my little brother, and it was how I described it in the last chapter. We ate dinner and caught up on each other's lives. He was adorable. His girlfriend—who he later married —came too. She cried when I hugged my brother.

I could tell he was happy to see me but not as happy as I was. At that table, I finally realized how differently I saw the situation as an adult.

Because he had been so young at the time of our dad's death, he'd dealt with our separation in his own way. It was a different loss for him. We spoke a few times over email after that, but I never saw him again. He didn't return my last email message, and I'm not sure why.

Acceptance has helped me to move on. I am not sad about him anymore. I love my brother, and I believe he loves me. We just live different lives, and I no longer pine over that little boy I missed so much. The grownup in me sends him love in my prayers, and I hope he knows I'm always here for him.

I finished my Master's degree when I returned from traveling. I've been writing and teaching in San Francisco ever since. The side waitressing job I got when I came home didn't help me lose weight because, of course, I spent a lot of time eating the profits. I did, however, eventually lose twenty pounds by exercising and (partially) eliminating crap from my diet.

I don't use men to fill my voids anymore. I date like a healthy woman and have filled that emptiness with a full life, love for myself, and a whole lot of other positive practices, like prayer, meditation, and being of service to others. Time—and getting comfortable in my skin—has shown me I no longer need strangers to take care of a problem they didn't create. When a man touches me now, it is simply because I want him to. No subtext.

I also quit using alcohol to mask, numb, and keep me from feeling the inevitable discomforts of my life, but that's another story, one I'm writing now.

I turned forty this year and felt an overwhelming sense of gratitude. Writing, dealing with my life as it comes, and staying in the moment the best I can have all helped me to cultivate joy I never knew possible. I still make a ton of mistakes, get frustrated, say stupid things, and beat myself up. The difference, now, is I can recognize when I am doing this and stop. Today, I feel content, which means I love who I see in the mirror, and I treat the people around me with that same love. It's simple and very imperfect. I believe there's a master plan for all of us. All I have to do is keep putting one foot in front of the other and find the silver lining, even when things don't go my way.

With so much love,

Michelle

PS. For more pictures and video from the trip, check out mkennedywriter.com.

Gratitude

THANK YOU, FIRST, to Shannon, for making the trip hilarious and fun. I love you from the bottom of my heart. Thank you for teaching me about relationships and for being there for me through this process. You always lift me up, and I'm here for you for eternity.

Thank you to my mother for always supporting me and for telling me at an early age that I can and will accomplish anything I set my mind to. Thank you also for proofreading this over and over again. Thank you, Maria Shriver and Lindsay Schnaidt, for believing in my work and for helping me to get the writing out of my computer and in front of other humans. Thank you to my beautiful writing coach, Kristy Lin Billuni, who held my hand, kept me on the train, and taught me so much. Finally, thank you to my attorney, Nicholas Jollymore, for guiding me and answering my five-thousand questions.

Thank you to everyone who supported this writing, read the book—or parts of it—and who gave me suggestions. Thank you for your encouragement during the incredible amount of time it took for me to release this thing: Matt DiGirolamo, Ryan and Sarah Kennedy, Jessica and Matt Cramer, Rebecca Heyman, Deborah and John Glerum, Julia Stuart, Michelle Chahine, Lauren Schutte, Dr. Corless Smith, Ann Connelly, Kayla Broughton, Roberta Gore, Charlene Quiram, Krystel Bell, Rachel Smith, Kristy Babb, Nicole Drago, Claire Bidwell Smith, Noa Daniels, Anne MacLaughlin, Ricardo Robinson, Kirby Timmons, Jaime Shea, Beverly Chrisman, Donald Hilland, Kimber Tiernan, Nicky Park, Nilima Patel, Katie Reed, Miles Horton, Haley Samuelson, Brendan Knapp and Lauren Griffin.

Author Photo Credit: Lisa Keating

Made in the USA
Middletown, DE
25 October 2016